# The Abingdon Women's Preaching Annual

Series 3
Year A

Compiled and Edited by

## *Beverly A. Zink-Sawyer*

Abingdon Press
Nashville

THE ABINGDON WOMEN'S PREACHING ANNUAL

*Copyright © 2004 by Abingdon Press*

*This book is printed on recycled, acid-free, elemental-chlorine–free paper.*

ISBN 0-687-09583-2
ISSN 1086-8240

04 05 06 07 08 09 10 11 12 13—10 9 8 7 6 5 4 3 2 1
MANUFACTURED IN THE UNITED STATES OF AMERICA

*For Steve, Phil, and Fraser*

*The men who love and support the women*

# Contents

# Introduction

Of the debates that have raged in homiletical circles in recent years one concerns the extent to which the preacher should refer to herself or himself in sermons. Some homileticians maintain that any self-reference in sermons deflects from the gospel message and should be avoided completely. Others believe that personal illustrations and self-disclosure serve to deepen the sincerity of the message and broaden the relationship between the preacher and the listeners, and therefore may be used appropriately and judiciously. As Fred Craddock reminds us, "Self-disclosure has a long and honorable history in the Scriptures."[1] The call from God that came to prophets of the Old Testament figured prominently in their proclamation. The apostle Paul frequently pointed to his own life as a model for the transformative work of God. Modern prophets such as Martin Luther King, Jr., used personal experience and private visions to inspire movements that changed the world.

In his textbook *The Witness of Preaching,* Tom Long suggests that the most descriptive image of the preacher is that of a witness who "is not authoritative because of rank or power but rather because of what the preacher has seen and heard."[2] Every preacher is—or should be—a witness to the truth of God's grace that has been experienced firsthand. The good news of Jesus Christ spread from obscure first-century villages in Palestine across the world and down through the centuries by means of the testimonies of those whose lives had been transformed by the gospel. Even in this age of sophisticated technology and communication, such personal testimony placed alongside the words of Scripture remains the most genuine means of pointing others toward Christian faith.

As I gathered the sermon briefs offered in this volume, I was struck by the faithful, careful, and beautiful ways in which these women preachers have used their own experiences to bear witness to the truth of the texts they proclaim. They neither obscure the message nor exploit their experiences. Instead, by means of personal experiences through which they have witnessed the grace of God, they invite us into a similar experience—and, more important, a similar insight into God's grace. Through Barbara MacHaffie's experience as a child lost in a department store, we come to know God as one who reaches down to dry our tears of sadness. In the charred woods surrounding Tina Cox's home after a brush fire, we see seeds of hope and new life. Through Susan Steinberg and her daughter's evening ritual of slathering peppermint foot lotion on each other's feet, we come to understand the intimacy of Jesus' act of washing his disciples' feet on his final night with them. Martha Moore-Keish explores the dangers and joys of our journey to the promised land as she witnesses her infant daughter's baptism. And when we are born of the Spirit, we view the world with new eyes, much as Jan Holton discovers an amazing clarity of vision through long overdue new glasses.

These are but a few of the personal experiences we are invited to share with the preachers included in this volume; and through their insights we gain new glimpses of the power and presence of God in our midst, and the truth of the gospel. So look, listen, feel, and discover with all these preachers the great riches of faith that surround us, and go out as witnesses to God's grace.

*Beverly A. Zink-Sawyer*
*Transfiguration of the Lord 2003*
*Richmond, Virginia*

1. Fred B. Craddock, *Preaching* (Nashville: Abingdon Press, 1985), 208.
2. Thomas G. Long, *The Witness of Preaching* (Louisville: Westminster John Knox Press, 1989), 44.

# First Sunday of Advent

## Jill Y. Crainshaw

---

**Isaiah 2:1-5:** Isaiah envisions the Lord's house and God's judgment upon the nations.

**Psalm 122:** The psalmist prays for the peace of Jerusalem.

**Romans 13:11-14:** Paul challenges Christian believers to "love one another" and live faithfully since the day of salvation is near.

**Matthew 24:36-44:** Matthew commands watchfulness for the coming of the Son of Man.

---

## REFLECTIONS

This year's lectionary texts invite unexpected sounds and colors to dance together on the canvas we call Advent. Voices in the wilderness. Falling stars. Melodies of celebration transposed into dissonant chords of lament. Advent is a season both stormy with eschatological (and sometimes apocalyptic) anticipation and exultant with promised presence.

The season of Advent historically emphasized the multiple "advents" of Christ (the remembered and often reenacted nativity, the promised second coming, and the persistent incarnational advent in Word and Sacrament). This suggests that Advent is not only, nor even primarily, a time of "waiting" for Christmas. That is one reason that the voices we hear in the texts for each of the Sundays in Advent, while they include sounds of festivity and praise, also echo hauntingly with the minor chords of lament, lament of unfulfilled hope that stands in stark contrast to the dancing carols of contemporary celebrations.

The eschatological language of Matthew 24 embodies this tension. Even as department stores glitter with Christmas cheer, the readings from Matthew draw the church toward discordant sounds of uncertainty and ambiguity. In this way, the ancient words of Matthew embody contemporary realities. People today live with terrifying questions, with unexplained suffering, and with unfulfilled expectations. The quartet of voices from the first Sunday in Advent can shape the contemporary community's way of living in the midst of dissonant realities in a stance of faith and action.

Matthew's picturesque call to wakefulness reminds us that language alone, voice alone, is not adequate to express what Advent anticipates. Rendering God's grace meaningfully in Advent involves both proclamation through language and proclamation through embodiment—the cedar scent of the Advent wreath, the growing "fire" of candles that marks the passing of time during the season, brushstrokes of purple or blue on a wilderness landscape. Undergirded by Matthew 24's Advent challenge, the liturgical preacher and the community are invited to use oral and visual arts to stir the imagination and to embody in worship and in actions of care in the world the promise that the "Word becomes flesh" in many unexpected advents.

# A SERMON BRIEF

## "Who Could Have Imagined It?"

Who could have imagined it? My friend never expected it, not in a million years. She sat in the parking lot that afternoon waiting for her husband to come out of the grocery store, something she'd done uneventfully dozens of times before. So she never expected *that* to happen while she was waiting. But there it was in the parking lot—a gargantuan Harley-Davidson motorcycle. Now, a motorcycle in a parking lot may be a rather ordinary sight, but this wasn't just any motorcycle because of what was sitting in a basket on the back of this monster machine. Well, my friend never expected to see what she saw that afternoon while she was waiting. There on the back of that Harley-Davidson sat none other than an equally gargantuan tomcat wearing a motorcycle helmet. The driver of the machine came out of the store. She had to ask. "That cat rides with you?"

"Yep. Goes with me everywhere. We just got here from Tennessee." With that, the driver put on his helmet, revved his engine, and drove away, both he and the cat leaning into the curve as they rounded the corner.

Advent. A season of waiting. But what is it, really, that we are waiting for, and do we really expect the unexpected? The questions become more persistent each year. What do the caroling sounds of our "Joy to the Worlds" mean to those people in New York City who watched their lives crumble in September 2001? What does the lullabying melody of "away in a manger, no crib for a bed" mean to refugee children in Pakistan? Even if all of that seems far away from our daily lives, few of us are immune to postholiday blues. December's gift-giving becomes January's Visa bills, and we wonder, "What was it, really, that we were waiting for?" Is it possible, can we at least hope that there is something more? Is it possible for something about God and faith that we could never have imagined, not in a million years, to rumble into our waiting to startle us and cause us to look at our world in new and life-changing ways?

The language of Matthew 24 is certainly not what most people expect to hear on the Sunday that begins the venerable four-Sunday "countdown to Christmas." (In my country-church Lutheran childhood the Advent wreath was a beloved way to mark time between Thanksgiving and Christmas Day.) On the first Sunday in Advent, we don't expect to hear about cosmic weather transformations. Stars spiraling down from the heavens. Mysterious disappearances. Trumpets and angels and swirling divine clouds. Choirs of angels showing up in the clouds to sing to kind-faced shepherds in the fields are familiar to us. But Matthew's meteorological sounds and colors of eschatological judgment are harsh to our ears. That could be why the language of today's text, verses 36-44, haunts us. What do Matthew's vivid images of what is out there just beyond our sight have to do with Advent waiting in 2004?

Matthew 24 was intended to startle the Matthean community awake to new ways of being in the world. God is coming, the words announce, not like a shepherd but like a thief. Be ready. These words of alarm on the first Sunday in Advent encroach on our nostalgic Christmas celebrations, disorienting us just when we're ready to sip hot chocolate, place baby Jesus in the manger on our fireplace hearth, and fondly (or not so fondly) remember the gentle (or not so gentle) ghosts of Christmases past. Standing in almost mischievous contrast, today's text opens the door to a holiday decor storage closet that we may prefer to keep closed. Could it be that during Advent we prepare for something that hasn't happened yet, something that threatens like a storm brewing on the horizon but that somehow brings peace and justice? We don't know exactly what this something looks like or when it will happen. Matthew only promises that it will happen.

Troubling, isn't it? Almost threatening and intrusive, this text's talk of floods and sudden disappearances. And yet, on this first Sunday of Advent, these vivid words strike a chord within us. The community of faith today also gathers in anticipation of a time of peace and justice beyond our wildest imaginings. Cats really do ride on motorcycles sometimes. Lions may one day lie down with lambs. God's creation is not ancient history, but unfinished story. In ways both seen and unseen, God's footsteps are still hollowing valleys out and raising mountains up.

And those kinds of promises are at the core of Advent waiting. We don't know what the future has in store, but experience teaches us. Tragedy shotguns into lives—the results of routine X-rays or a long-distance phone call. The interstate highway we call life can become narrow and treacherous. Sometimes we strain our eyes and our hearts to catch sight of God's face in it all but can only see darkness, trouble, ghosts, and pain. Matthew 24 asks us to keep watching, to be alert to the unseen mysteries in the ordinary stuff all around us, to expect the unexpected. Things are on their way that no one could ever have imagined, not in a million years.

# SUGGESTIONS FOR WORSHIP

Advent liturgies can be powerfully incarnational. The liturgy for this season potentially does two important things: (1) it provides the cradle out of which preaching grows, and (2) it gives shape to the body through which the Word goes out. In Advent liturgies, Word is voice, vision, and action.

## Call to Worship (based on Psalm 122)

LEADER:  "I was glad when they said to me, 'Let us go to the house of the Lord!'"

PEOPLE:  **Our feet are standing in your house, O God. We gather
to sing,
to dance,
to weep,
to listen,**

14

to wonder,
to catch sight of your face in our midst.

LEADER: Guide our footsteps toward new visions of your justice and truth.

PEOPLE: **Give us the courage to watch with new eyes.**

LEADER: Awaken our ears to unexpected melodies of hope and peace.

PEOPLE: **"I was glad when they said to me, 'Let us go to the house of the Lord!' " We are here. Come, Lord Jesus.**

# Prayer of Reflection

God of the unexpected, winter is creeping into cities and country forests. Oaks and maples are almost bare, only their bony winter fingers drawing a map against the sky. Give us courage, the innate courage of the woodland, O God, to bare our souls to you during this season of waiting. Shine your light on our lives and clothe us in the colors of your presence. Make room in our hearts for the unexpected possibilities only your grace can give.

# Prayer for Illumination

O God, as your Word drenched the darkness with light in the beginning, may our hearing of your Word today drench our hearts with eager anticipation of the light of eternal hope. Amen.

# Second Sunday of Advent

### Claire Smith

---

**Isaiah 11:1-10:** Isaiah foretells a peaceful kingdom that will follow the coming of the one anointed by the Spirit of the Lord.

**Psalm 72:1-7, 18-19:** The psalmist prays that justice and righteousness will characterize the king's reign.

**Romans 15:4-13:** Paul prays that believers in Rome will be granted steadfastness in their faith.

**Matthew 3:1-12:** John the Baptist proclaims God's coming kingdom and calls the people to a baptism of repentance.

---

## REFLECTIONS

While I was reflecting on Matthew 3:1-12, the theme "preparing for a momentous event" emerged. During the season of Advent, we are focused on a momentous event: the great event of Christmas. But what is Advent really about? Those of us who understand its true meaning know that Advent is about preparation: preparation for the coming of Christ and all that his coming means for our lives. It is also about looking backward and forward. We look back to the birth of the Christ Child and the new kingdom he initiated in the world, and we look forward to Christ's second coming when that kingdom will be realized. And both advents demand our attention and our preparations.

In the Gospel text, Matthew offers clues and guidelines for our preparations during Advent. We are introduced to John the herald, who prepared the way for Jesus. John does not simply announce that something great is imminent; he also gives some idea of the significance of this event and what it requires. He lets people know they need to prepare, and he shows them how to do it. Thus he proclaims,

"Repent, for the kingdom of heaven has come near." He calls them to "prepare" through repentance and works of righteousness. And if one does not participate in this preparation there are consequences, because for John the coming kingdom is an imperative.

Although the season of Advent is often lost in our focus on Christmas, on the birth of Christ, John's proclamation calls us to an important prior reflection on what we should prepare *for.* We are not simply preparing to welcome a baby, but a king—a king who has come and set forth the demands upon those who desire to be part of his kingdom, and a king who will come again. Are we prepared? As we attempt to answer that question, may we examine our lives and seek to bring them closer to the standards of this new kingdom as we commit ourselves anew to this king.

# A SERMON BRIEF

## "Preparation for What?"

Advent is a time of great excitement and anticipation. It is also a time of grand preparation. Each of us is preparing in some way. We have begun. Even those of us who leave many of our preparations until Christmas Eve are preparing mentally. In my own Guyanese context, this preparation has an aspect of newness. It is not unusual to acquire new furniture, new clothing, and other new items, or even to apply new paint to fix up our homes in preparations for Christmas. Our preparation also has a culinary aspect as we prepare the special delicacies associated with the Christmas season. Some of these require hours, some even days, of work. And of course there is the shopping experience that figures large in our preparations. All of this preparation seems to begin around the end of November. When that time comes and the Christmas advertisements and songs begin, it is as if we have heard the call that heralds a great event. The media call to us, "Christmas is coming!" The commercial sector calls to us, "Christmas is coming!" Everybody calls out, "Christmas is coming!" But what is this event, and how do we prepare for it as disciples of Jesus Christ?

On this second Sunday of Advent, we continue to prepare for the Great Event. It is an event that is rooted in but goes beyond both Advent and Christmas as we look back to the birth of Christ and forward to the day when Christ will come again. We hear anew the call of John the Baptist in Matthew 3:

17

Repent for the kingdom of heaven has come near. . . .
"The voice of one crying out in the wilderness:
'Prepare the way of the Lord,
make his paths straight.' "

Christ came. At Christmas we celebrate his birth. But we believe that Christ will come again. The kingdom, the reign of God, is yet to be fully realized—a reign of justice, peace, and righteousness as embodied in Isaiah 11:1-10. Christ will return and usher in this kingdom in its fullness. It will be a time of deliverance and grace, yes. But it will also be a time of judgment. Hence the call that demands our active response.

It is a call that comes in the midst of all the other calls that come to us. It is a call that clamors for our attention. A Christmas song speaks of the busyness of rushing about with our Christmas treasures while hearing the sound of silver bells. But what do you hear? Can you hear the voice that says "Repent?" This is what we are called to do in this Advent season. As we read Matthew 3:1-12, we recognize the call to confess and repent—confess where we have been going wrong, where our lives depart from how God intends us to live, and confess our faith in Jesus Christ. Then we are led to act upon this confession in our deeds of repentance. This call comes to everyone and stands in stark contrast to the "magic" of Christmas that leads our focus away from the worship of God in Christ to the external trappings of Christmas. Ultimately, it is a call of preparation.

Confession and repentance as our preparation require concrete evidence—"fruit worthy of repentance," as Scripture says. They are more than verbal professions. As we recognize and confess where our lives have gone out of alignment, our repentance moves us to get those lives in line with God's kingdom principles of justice, peace, and righteousness. Only this will suffice. Where the Jews were concerned, the Scriptures reveal, their lineage from Abraham would not suffice. Neither will the toil and faithfulness of those who have gone before us suffice for us. Our active participation in Christ's new kingdom is required. Luke 3:8-14 tells us what "fruit [is] worthy of repentance." The phrase refers to specific daily practices. Wherever we are located we are called to act with honesty, fairness, and integrity, not using one's position of advantage to oppress. These are God's standard of righteousness, and only these will lead to satisfaction and peace. We begin with how we treat each other every day: our attitude toward our community; how we treat each other at home; how we treat each other in our workplaces; how we treat each other as we go about our busy lives in the world (as when we encounter long lines and impatient people this holiday season!).

The Advent call of God places before us an opportunity to prepare anew for the coming of Christ, to live lives that bear fruit that reflect our repentance. How will we respond to this gracious opportunity? Are we listening to the call that encourages us to confess and repent, to constantly align ourselves according to God's standard? Are we preparing by living out in our lives the "kingdom values" embodied by Christ? What do you need to do this Advent season? What will you do?

# SUGGESTIONS FOR WORSHIP

## Call to Worship (from Psalm 72:1-7, 18, 19 and Romans 15:11)

| | |
|---|---|
| LEADER: | God of justice and righteousness, |
| **PEOPLE:** | **You call us to worship you.** |
| LEADER: | May we sing your praises with one voice. |
| **PEOPLE:** | **May all the peoples praise you.** |
| LEADER: | Blessed be the name of the Lord! |
| **PEOPLE:** | **May God's glory fill the earth** |
| **ALL:** | **From this time and forever, Amen.** |

## Prayer of Confession (from Psalm 72:1-7 and Romans 15:5)

Almighty God, we confess our failures and shortcomings. We desire what is easy and convenient rather than that which is right and just in your sight. Too often we ignore the poor and unwittingly assist in oppressing the weak. We fail to follow the path of peace. As we prepare for your Son's rule of righteousness and justice, forgive us our neglect and help us to glorify you in all that we do and say. In Jesus' name we pray.

## Assurance of Pardon

Our Merciful God welcomes us and as we have confessed our sins, forgives us, through Christ Jesus our Lord.

# Benediction

May the God of mercy and hope, the Servant Son, and the Spirit of Wisdom and Understanding guide you as you prepare for the coming of the Lord and in the ways you live in this world with each other and with all of God's creation.

# Third Sunday of Advent

Maggie Lauterer

---

Isaiah 35:1-10: The prophet predicts the return of God's people to Zion, where the desert will blossom and the glory of the Lord will be revealed.

Luke 1:46*b*-55: Mary sings her song of praise.

James 5:7-10: Believers are urged to be patient in their sufferings as they await the coming of the Lord.

Matthew 11:2-11: John the Baptist sends messengers to ascertain Jesus' identity.

---

## REFLECTIONS

In my Bible (NRSV), Isaiah 35 is subtitled "The Return of the Redeemed to Zion." It seems to me that nothing could be more appropriate for Advent than the language of returning. But what is returning? The joy of the healed heart is told in language of a barren land returning to wholeness and blooming. The King James Version of a verse in this chapter—"the desert shall rejoice, and blossom as the rose"—inspired the beloved old German carol "Lo, How a Rose E'er Blooming."

As we read Isaiah 35 in the midst of winter, not far from the longest night of the year, it is a radical departure from winter reality to think of a rose blooming. Perhaps that is the strong message of this chapter: the contrasts of barrenness and bloom, of blind and sighted, of deaf and hearing, and of the tongue of the speechless singing for joy.

## A SERMON BRIEF

There is nothing like pain. And in the middle of the night, there is nothing so lonely as being in pain.

21

One December night not long ago, I had the misfortune of damaging my left eye's cornea with a contact lens. During the emergency visit to the doctor that cold evening, he told me my eye looked more like chopped liver than a human orb. I agreed it felt that way. He had only two tablets of pain medicine at his office that night, so he gave them to me and wrote a prescription to fill in the morning. I gulped them down and waited for relief as I lay down to sleep.

At two o'clock in the morning, I awoke in excruciating pain. The medicine had worn off, and there was no more to take. I lay there, listening to the howling December wind outside my bedroom window and to the old furnace downstairs cranking up to combat the cold. While the pain in my head throbbed and the wind whistled, I thought about the wilderness of pain, the desert of darkness, and the barrenness of heart within me. *This is temporary,* I told myself. I can get pain medicine first thing in the morning. But as I lay in dark and hurt, I thought of those feelings of barrenness we all suffer, for which, even first thing in the morning, there is no simple relief.

We all must deal with those barren, painful places within us; but first we must acknowledge and find them. To do that, we must take a trip across our own interior landscapes. Let's travel down the paths, past the nice places where there are flowers blooming and trickling, splashing summer-day waterfalls. Those are the parts of ourselves we like and enjoy. Those are our better parts, the parts we point to with pride and joy and satisfaction. But further down the path we come to the hidden deserts and wilderness places. Those are places often not visible from the outside. We may even deny to the outside world that they exist.

We all have them. A place where it hurts to go—be it a painful, damaging memory, or a loss, or a part of us that we can't control or understand. Perhaps it is a fear, a hatred, a resentment. Those are desert spots, dry and barren within us, but affecting all of our being. It could even be a place like the astronomer's theoretical black hole, which, with a power unchecked, pulls in everything around it. These dark, powerful places can overpower and bring the physical feelings of helplessness described by Isaiah as "weak hands" and "feeble knees" and "a fearful heart."

Isaiah sets the desperate tone in the first words of chapter 35: "The wilderness and the dry land." Those who have witnessed desert land—or a severe drought for that matter—understand what barren means. But it was different in the deserts Isaiah knew. The land lay dry and dead and seemingly without hope of green life. But even in that dry, tortured land, the rains must inevitably come.

There is a season in the desert expressed in Hebrew as *p'rach,* which translates as "burst forth" And when those clouds bring an end to the dry season, showers of rain arrive. Then, almost literally overnight, the hidden and patient seeds and roots, waiting under the fertile but parched soil of the Middle East, burst into color and coolness and life where only the day before there was a barren place. The life was already there waiting. Waiting for the rain.

We all have dry, barren places waiting for the coming of God's cool, soothing rains.

Verses 1 and 2 of Isaiah 35 describe dry and barren land bursting into the blossom of the "chavazelet," the Hebrew flower named. The King James Version translated "chavazelet" to "rose." The New Revised Standard Version calls it a "crocus." Those who have experienced the deserts Isaiah described know there is a little flower that bursts into bloom in the *p'rach* after the long-sought rains. They can change a sandy, tan landscape into exquisite color and life.

In the pain of my aching cornea in the middle of that Advent night, I could not help thinking of the old fifteenth-century German carol I love:

> Lo, how a Rose e'er blooming from tender stem hath sprung!
> Of Jesse's lineage coming, as those of old have sung.
> It came, a floweret bright, amid the cold of winter,
> When half spent was the night.
> Isaiah 'twas foretold it, the Rose I have in mind;
> With Mary we behold it, the Virgin Mother kind.
> To show God's love aright, she bore to us a Savior,
> When half spent was the night.

In darkness, in barrenness of soul, in parched heart, Isaiah gives the dry, barren, desert places of our lives the hope of *p'rach*—the bursting forth of life made whole—bringing the deaf heart to hear, the blind heart to see, the lame heart to leap like a deer, and the heart's tongue to sing for joy. When we think there's no hope for that aching desert place inside, we read Isaiah and hear him foretell: "He will come and save you."

This Christmas, what desert land within, what parched place in a soul, what lost cove in an interior landscape cries out for the *p'rach* of birth? Where in the interior landscape would you invite Christ to be born, to heal, and to save? Christmas comes to remind us that Christ is waiting to be born there.

# SUGGESTIONS FOR WORSHIP

## Call to Worship (based on Isaiah 35:8-10)

LEADER: A highway through the desert has been promised for us to travel.

PEOPLE: **It shall be for God's people where no one will go astray.**

LEADER: It is a highway through the desert to the heart of God.

PEOPLE: **The people of God will come singing, with everlasting joy.**

LEADER: The people shall obtain joy and gladness.

PEOPLE: **Sorrow and sighing shall flee away.**

ALL: **In this promise, we know that Christ is coming! He is the narrow way to lead us home. Amen.**

## Prayer of Confession

O Lord of all, hear our prayer. We come to confess that we have deserts in our lives, and we have guarded them from you. In the worst of wildernesses, we have often kept your rains from healing our parched lives. We protect from your healing the dry, barren places of scaly anger and resentments, fear and anxiety.

Come close, Lord, and forgive us our sins, that we may long for and accept the deep-cleansing rains of your mercy. Bring our hearts into bloom like the fresh, bright flowers in the desert after the long-awaited rain. In the name of Jesus we pray. Amen.

## Assurance of Pardon (based on Revelation 22)

LEADER: The river of the water of life, bright as crystal, flows from the throne of God. We are washed in its waters, and brought to life through the Lamb of God, Jesus Christ.

PEOPLE: **The servants of God and the Lamb will worship him and see his face, and his name will be marked on their foreheads.**

ALL: **Thanks be to God!**

*December 12, 2004*

# Benediction

And now may the Lord, who brings the rain of righteousness, flow into the deserts of our lives and bring us into everlasting bloom through the cleansing grace of the Holy Child of God, Jesus Christ. Amen.

# Fourth Sunday of Advent

Denise Bennett

---

**Isaiah 7:10-16:** Isaiah assures King Ahaz of a sign of the coming of Immanuel.

**Psalm 80:1-7, 17-19:** The psalmist prays for the restoration of Israel and its people.

**Romans 1:1-7:** Paul declares his faith in Jesus Christ for the believers at Rome.

**Matthew 1:18-25:** Matthew tells of the birth of Jesus the Messiah.

---

## REFLECTIONS

A few years ago my mother-in-law gave my husband, Jim, a lovely framed pastel entitled "Sleepy Joe." It shows Joseph snoozing as he holds a sleeping baby Jesus. It is a tender depiction of the character who often gets lost in the shuffle in the Christmas story. The drawing also reminds me of a picture I took of Jim dozing in the rocking chair, holding one of our sleeping infant sons. Both images help me connect to Joseph in this passage from Matthew. As a storyteller, and as a woman, I have always been more attracted to stories about Jesus' beginnings in the Gospel of Luke. The story in Matthew is terse, and while it is focused on Joseph, we don't find out much about him except that he is a righteous man, as his decision not to publicly divorce Mary demonstrates. Joseph's age and occupation are not stated anywhere in Scripture. However, John Pilch points out in *The Cultural World of Jesus: Sunday by Sunday, Cycle A* (p. 11) that the way Joseph receives his information from God may contain a clue to his age. In Joel 2:28, the prophet tells us that "old men shall dream dreams, and . . . young men shall see visions." Taking that into account, I decided to portray Joseph as an older man, and therefore (probably) a widower. Perhaps, too, my work as a chaplain in a home for elders influenced my portrayal of Joseph. I know several widowers who, though deeply grieved by their wives' deaths, have continued to nurture others through their ministry. They are men graced by God with incredible patience and faith, as is Joseph in the story. They have been an inspiration to me. Their lifelong love and obedience to God—what the scripture calls "righteousness"—remind me daily of the most important thing in this story: Emmanuel is born to us. God is with us.

# A SERMON BRIEF

Joseph brushed the sawdust from his hands and began to put his tools away. Mallet, adz, bow saw, and chisel were put into their proper places, as if ordering his things would order his thoughts, his heart. Finding ways to solve problems in his work, to join pieces of wood together smoothly, gave him great satisfaction; but the problem he faced now was not like his work. He had found the solution to it, but it gave no satisfaction, only pain. In the room next door, his oldest daughter had the evening meal ready, but tonight he had no appetite. The news he had heard this morning was too upsetting.

After his wife had died, he thought that he would not marry again, but the relatives pushed him. "Joseph, you are not so old, you need a wife. Who will take care of you when your daughter marries? Who will take care of your other children?" At last, a match was made for him with a young cousin, Mary. Though men and women not married to one another did not mingle, he'd had a glimpse of her now and again. A pretty girl with large dark eyes; there was something in those eyes that he could not define. A promise? Well, if it had been a promise it was one that had been given to someone else, for just this morning another cousin, Eli, who was married to the nosiest woman in town, had come to tell him the news: Mary, Joseph's betrothed, was pregnant. "Oh such shame has come on our family," Eli moaned. "What are you going to do about this, Joseph?" Joseph just stood there looking at him; dumb as a block of wood, Joseph thought now. Finally he said, "Thank you for telling me, Eli. Now excuse me, I have work to do."

He was angry and disappointed. He and Mary were to be married at the end of the year. How he had been longing for her to become his wife. He was, he admitted to himself, lonely. Though his first marriage was arranged, as this one was—as all marriages were—he and his wife had been blessed. Their love for each other had grown through the years. When she had died, Joseph grieved deeply. When he finally agreed to the betrothal to Mary, it had surprised him to feel hope and desire surging in him again. Not an old dried-up stick after all. But now this. It was a great affront to his honor, but even so he had decided that he would not divorce her publicly. According to the law, he could have demanded that she be stoned; but no, he would not do that to her. That might be some men's understanding of righteousness, but it was not his.

He finished up in the shop and went into the next room. His daughter brought him a bowl of stew and some bread, but he hardly touched it. The other children prattled about this and that, but he did not pay much attention. Finally he pushed his bowl away and went to bed.

Lying there in the dark, listening to the night sounds, he remembered words that his father Jacob had spoken long ago: "Whether you are working with wood or with people, the Lord will provide a way to overcome your difficulties, but you must have patience and you must have faith." Jacob had demonstrated that every day of his life, but now Joseph thought that all the faith in the world could not undo the fact that Mary would no longer be his. He hoped that when he relinquished his claim to her, the father of her child would claim her. Oh, how the tongues of the village gossips would wag! He dreaded hearing them. He lay there for a long time, staring into the darkness until finally he drifted into sleep.

At first all Joseph could see was light, blinding light, then gradually it assumed a form, though the edges were not defined. It had no face, it had no mouth that he could see; all the same it spoke to him and he understood.

"Joseph, Son of David, do not be afraid to take Mary as your wife . . . 'They shall name him Emmanuel,' which means, "God is with us."

And then suddenly the light was gone.

The words "God is with us" were still echoing in Joseph's mind when he sat up in bed. He could hardly believe that it had been a dream. Somehow it had been more real than when he was awake. Mary, pregnant by the Holy Spirit—that was what the angel had said. But why would God entrust this child Jesus, this savior, to someone like him? A Galilean carpenter, a hick from the sticks. He wasn't wealthy or learned in the law, and he was no longer young. He remembered when his other children had been babies. So tiny, so fragile in his big callused hands. Would this child be the same? How would he raise such a boy? It seemed impossible. And then Joseph remembered the angel's last words; "They shall call him Emmanuel, which means 'God is with us.' " If God wanted him to do this, to wed Mary and to raise this child, then God would be with them. God had promised, and it would be so.

At first light, Joseph got up. Today he would tell Mary's family and his that he wanted to move the wedding date up. O how the tongues would wag! Well, they would wag whatever he did. Joseph had been given a task, and though he hardly felt prepared for it, somehow he would find a way to fulfill it. His father was right: by the grace of God, all difficulties could be overcome, if only one had patience and faith. Yes, patience and faith were the tools he needed. God would provide.

# SUGGESTIONS FOR WORSHIP

| | |
|---|---|
| ONE: | Dreamers, awaken! |
| **MANY:** | **God is with us!** |
| ONE: | Tiny and fragile, |
| **MANY:** | **God is with us!** |
| ONE: | Promise of angels, |
| **MANY:** | **God is with us!** |
| ONE: | Love never ending, |
| **ALL:** | **God is with us! Worship the one who dwells with us!** |

## Prayer of Confession

Dear God, we are not righteous like Joseph most of the time. When we think we have been wronged, we desire revenge and punishment. When you come to us, calling us to set aside our presumptions, to believe and to do what seems foolish in the eyes of the world, we turn away. We are more interested in the coming sales for Christmas shopping than in the coming of Emmanuel. Forgive us, God. Make us merciful, even as you are merciful. Help us to open our eyes to the truth of your love. Give us the faith to believe and the courage to obey, even when it is difficult. Help us to remember that the coming of the Christ Child is the real "reason for the season." In Jesus' name. Amen.

## Assurance of Pardon

In the name of the one who came to dwell among us, we are forgiven. Thanks be to God.

## Benediction

Listen to your dreams, watch for angels, know that you are not alone. God is with you; now go in peace. Amen.

# Christmas Eve

### Margaret Grun Kibben

---

**Isaiah 9:2-7:** The dark years of walking and waiting have ended. The burdens and oppression have been redeemed. The zeal of the Lord of hosts is unleashed in the birth of this child in whom all titles of authority are fulfilled. Justice and righteousness are his legacy.

**Psalm 96:** Honor, majesty, strength, and beauty surround the King. The earth, the heavens, and the elements proclaim the majesty of the Lord God. Come, sing, for the Lord comes to judge with righteousness and truth.

**Titus 2:11-14:** The life and death of Jesus Christ has redeemed us from all that is shameful and sinful, and freed us to live lives that are faithful and hopeful. This is the grace of God.

**Luke 2:1-14 (15-20):** Ordinary people are rocked by extraordinary events. And they respond with obedience, submitting their whole selves to the events unfolding before them. They walk in faith, uncertain of the future toward which they go. And it is the small child in the manger who changes their lives in ways they could never have imagined.

---

## REFLECTIONS

Each of these lectionary passages proclaims the good news that is ours this evening. God, who has the earth as his footstool, the heavens at his command, and the awe and majesty due to the most powerful, has chosen to be in relationship with us. God's grand design includes the promise of our salvation. The psalmist sings with grand voice that the hope is ours. The prophet proclaims with audacity that this hope is to be found in a child who will comfortably wear titles

31

that are set aside for the most revered of monarchs. Angels proclaim that this child is worthy of praise from the highest heavens.

But it is the gospel story that reminds us that the advent of our salvation is proclaimed to those of lowly estate. The power of God is unleashed in the humble birth of a child that we may come to understand that it is not by virtue of our circumstance or condition, and not due to our worth or works, but because of God's grace that God demonstrates the power of his love for his creation in the birth of his Son, Jesus the Christ.

# A SERMON BRIEF

The invitations had been distributed, even if they were sent out a little unconventionally. The message was shared by word-of-mouth, and in middle of the night. There was no RSVP indicated, but the appeal to the heart of the recipients was strong. Furthermore, there was nothing indicated as to what to wear or what to bring. But perhaps the most unusual fact regarding these invitations were the guests to whom they were addressed. Those who were summoned were considered the dregs of society, the least deserving of anything this special. These were shepherds after all, people who made their meager living among livestock, people who needed much latitude (read: distance) when considering their social graces (read: manners, dress, and more particularly, odor).

Unusual invitations make for unusual responses. These men who had spent their whole lives in that field, whose primary responsibility was to that flock of sheep, whose humble earnings were utterly dependent on the constant care and protection of these lowly animals, left their posts and responded to the summons. They were completely taken by the good news, and they gave up all that they knew, all that they had, and hurried to the life-changing event.

It makes for a beautiful and dramatic story. The promises, the prophecies, are all fulfilled on a starlit night as angels break into the ordinariness of life. And members of the least of society provide the ultimate example of faithfulness, grasping the significance of the invitation and responding with unfettered joy and reckless abandon.

More than mere drama, however, this story creates a dilemma. Not only does it provide a narrative with universal appeal, but it proclaims a timeless message: the promises, the prophecies, are meant also for us. As we read this scripture this evening we hear more than a quaint tale. Instead, we hear the angels break forth in great reverie and summon us to participate in this same event, with the same zeal and commitment demonstrated by the main characters.

Our response, however, is fraught with reserve and hesitance. We look at the back of the invitation to see if it was produced by Hallmark. We look around to see who else got one and to determine if their company is worth sharing. Or when considering our response, we waver, overwhelmed by our unworthiness. After all, who are we to be invited? We who have lived shameful lives? We who have never shared in such an event before? Even if we can overcome these hindrances, we may find ourselves reluctant to attend simply because we're much too busy to drop everything and attend the event of a lifetime.

The truth is, however, that not only are we expected to come, and come immediately, but that we are to arrive unencumbered. There is no room for preconceived notions, expectations or formalities, fear, shame, or reserve. This is a night of miracles and not of plans; a night of grace and not of judgment. There is nothing to prepare, no need to worry. We are to come just as we are. The invitation has been issued to all, including those who feel unworthy, and especially those who seem to be the least likely guests. Christmas is a time for beggars. It is meant for those who come with a hole in their hearts, and hurt in their lives. It will not disappoint those who arrive willing to receive the wholeness, healing, and salvation that God has chosen to give us as we celebrate the birth of his son, Jesus the Christ.

# SUGGESTIONS FOR WORSHIP

## Call to Worship (based on Psalm 96)

LEADER: Ascribe to the Lord, O families of the peoples, ascribe to the Lord glory and strength.

**PEOPLE: Honor and majesty are before God; strength and beauty are in God's sanctuary.**

LEADER: Ascribe to the Lord the glory due God's name.

**PEOPLE: Great is the Lord, and greatly to be praised.**

LEADER: Worship the Lord in holy splendor. Say among the nations, "The Lord is King!"

# Prayer of Confession and Assurance of Pardon

ALL:     **Gracious God, on this evening of awe and wonder, we find ourselves overwhelmed and fearful. Our daily routines have become tedious; our view of the world limited and self-serving. And the idea of change brings us fear and anxiety. How could anything good come from our feeble efforts anyway? Break into our lives this night and remind us of your grace. Tell us good tidings that we may know of your love for the least deserving. Guide us to discover the hope that you offer each of us in Jesus Christ.**

LEADER:  Do not be afraid; I bring you good news of great joy for all people. For unto you is born this day in the city of David, a Savior, who is Christ the Lord.

# Benediction

To all of us who are the least and the lost, the weary and the unfaithful, God's grace has been given to us this night. For unto us a child has been born, unto us a son is given. All authority rests on his shoulders; and he is named Wonderful Counselor, Mighty God, Everlasting Father, Prince of Peace.

# Christmas Day

Beverly A. Zink-Sawyer

---

**Isaiah 52:7-10:** The Lord has comforted and redeemed Jerusalem.

**Psalm 98:** The psalmist invites all of creation to join in praising the God "who has done marvelous things."

**Hebrews 1:1-4 (5-12):** In these last days, God has spoken to us by a Son.

**John 1:1-14:** The Word has become flesh in Jesus Christ.

---

## REFLECTIONS

A number of Protestant churches that once focused their Christmas celebrations primarily on Christmas Eve have added a service on Christmas Day. Whether it is one of lessons and carols or of Word and Table, a Christmas Day worship service affords faith communities a wonderful opportunity to move from the promises of Advent to the realization of Christmas hope. The lections appointed for Christmas Day remind us that Christ has indeed come and that God's work of salvation is forever in our midst to shine light into our darkness, to forge a way of hope through our deserts of despair, and to proclaim peace where war and strife seem to be the only ways of relating to one another. The meditation below is designed to lead to the Table where we encounter in a unique way the reality of God's Word spoken for all time in Jesus Christ.

## A SERMON BRIEF

One of the most successful advertising campaigns of the end of the twentieth century was the one featuring Joe Isuzu. You might remember old Joe; he's the guy who tried to sell us a new Isuzu automobile by making all kinds of preposterous claims about it—like the fact that it can carry a whole football team, or can climb Mount Everest, or that the Queen of England owns one. And this amazing car can be yours for only sixty-nine, ninety-five—dollars and cents, that is. While Joe Isuzu was speaking, the truth flashed in words at the bottom of the TV screen, making disclaimers such as "He's lying," and "It can only carry four passengers comfortably," and "The cost is really six *thousand,* nine-hundred and ninety-five *dollars.*" Joe always concluded his pitch with the same trademark phrase: "You have my word on it."

We laugh because we know how reliable Joe's word is. But maybe ours is the laughter of recognition, perhaps with a twinge of guilt. For we all know how easy it is to "give our word"—and how hard it is to keep it. Think of all the times you've "given your word" to someone. If you are married, you gave your word to your spouse in the form of wedding vows spoken before God and a church full of witnesses. Those of you who are parents probably presented your child for baptism before a congregation—and you gave your word to raise your child as a disciple of Jesus Christ. Those of us who are ordained gave our word to serve God and the church as faithful ministers and church leaders. We pledge our love, our loyalty, our very lives with our words.

But talk is cheap, as AT&T and its competitors continually remind us. Words have in fact lost some of the power and significance they once had. Imagine going down the road to your local bank and telling them that you'll give your word that you'll pay your mortgage each month. I don't think so. We've all been burned by words that haven't been kept. Keeping one's word doesn't seem to be quite as easy as it once was. I stood before hundreds of couples while I served as a pastor and witnessed them giving their words to each other in the form of wedding vows. But I know the statistics, and probably half of them will not keep their words, and their marriages will end in divorce. Countless people stand before congregations all across the country, promising to be faithful members. But why are our churches only one-third full on Sunday mornings? And why are so many churches losing members and closing their doors at an alarming rate? Where are all the people who gave their word when they joined the church? And how about those parents who were so eager to have their children baptized, who promised to raise their children in the knowledge and love of God and in the fellowship of the church? If they had kept their word, we'd be putting up new Sunday school buildings left and right. And yes, even those of us who took vows of ordination sometimes find them difficult to keep. The demands of ministry are great; sometimes we just can't do all that is expected of us.

Yes, it's easy to give our word—but keeping our word is another story. We may be forced to break our promises. Things change; people change; we change. We are human, and sometimes our word fails us.

Into our world of failed words and broken promises this Christmas Day comes the Word given for all time: "In the beginning was the Word, and the Word was with God, and the Word was God. . . . And the Word became flesh and lived among us, . . . full of grace and truth" (John 1:1, 14). This was not the first time God had spoken: *davar Yahweh,* the word of the Lord, echoed throughout the Old Testament. God's word brought all creation into being: "And God said, 'Let there be light,' and there was light." During the Exodus, God's word was written on the tablets of the Law and given to the people through Moses. Later in Israel's history, God's word came through the prophets, calling the people to repent and to live righteously.

But God's word was always incomplete until the coming of Christ. "Long ago God spoke to our ancestors in many and various ways by the prophets," the writer to the Hebrews tells us, "but in these last days [God] has spoken to us by a Son" (1:1-2*a*). "The Word became flesh and lived among us, . . . full of grace and truth." Here was a word kept after centuries of promises,—a word written not on stone tablets but on the heart; a word spoken for all time.

Once again on this Christmas Day, we hear that Word anew. It's not an "abracadabra" kind of word; not a word that, when spoken, will make all our heartaches disappear and all our dreams come true. No. It's something even better: it's a "pitch-a-tent-and-hang-in-there-with-us" kind of word, as the Greek text states. It is many words, actually. It's a word of *hope* amidst the despair that threatens to undo us in these days of fear and uncertainty. It's a word of *encouragement* that inspires us to put one foot in front of the other as we step out in faith into God's promised future. It's a word of *strength* that enables us to keep *our* words to one another—and to God—even when that is not easy. Best of all, it is the Word that will have the *last word.* As Martin Luther put it in his great hymn, "one little word" shall fell the prince of darkness and all the rage he threatens to unleash upon us.

37

That "one little word," the Word uttered by God in Jesus Christ for all time, stands above all earthly powers and strengthens us with the Spirit and the gifts that are ours in Christ.

We gather around this holy table on this holy day to share God's gifts of bread and wine. We wait to hear God speak to us once again. Some of us come with skepticism, for we are so used to broken promises, so used to hearing human words that have not been kept. But here we partake of the reminders of the one Word that will never fail: the Word made flesh, full of grace and truth. So come, feast, and hear the voice of God echoing through our communion, saying, "You have my Word on it." Thanks be to God.

# SUGGESTIONS FOR WORSHIP

## Call to Worship (based on Isaiah 52)

LEADER: How beautiful upon the mountains are the feet of the messenger who announces peace,

PEOPLE: **Who brings good news, who announces salvation, who says to Zion, "Your God reigns."**

LEADER: Lift up your voices, sing together for joy!

PEOPLE: **For the Lord has comforted the people; God has redeemed Jerusalem.**

LEADER: God has revealed God's holy arm before the eyes of all the nations;

PEOPLE: **And all the ends of the earth shall see the salvation of our God.**

## Benediction

Go out into the world in joy on this Christmas Day, in the power and presence of God's Word spoken for all time in Jesus Christ our Lord. Amen.

# Epiphany of the Lord

### Tina Cox

---

**Isaiah 60:1-6:** The light has come, and all nations shall be drawn to the brightness of the dawn.

**Psalm 72:1-7, 10-14:** The psalmist prays for a king who will rule with justice and righteousness.

**Ephesians 3:1-12:** Paul tells of his ministry among the Gentiles.

**Matthew 2:1-12:** Wise men from the East seek the child born in Bethlehem.

---

## REFLECTIONS

Epiphany is a significant event in the church year, marking both a day and a season. Celebrated as the time when the light of Christ is made known to the Gentiles, it is a time rich in the symbolism of light. We find the symbolism of light in the texts from Isaiah ("Arise, shine for your light has come") and from Matthew (the light of the star). We also find implicit references to light in the Ephesians text ("reveal," "see"). Epiphany is also a time rich in narrative, because of the Matthean story of the Magi. It is this narrative of the wise men that I would offer up to my congregation, with an emphasis on Christ as the light of the world.

I believe that Matthew in his Gospel story of the Magi was trying to tell us of the cosmic significance of the birth of Christ—a turning point for the whole world. I am reminded of the words of T. S. Eliot, who spoke of the incarnation as "the still point of the turning world,"[1] and "the intersection of the timeless moment."[2] Eliot's words resonated with me when I reread an article by Joel Garreau in the *Washington Post* about "hinge moments in history."[3] I believe the incarnation was just such a hinge moment. That's what Matthew is describing in his nativity narratives.

While understanding the cosmic nature of God's grace in Jesus Christ, Matthew also understood that grace in individual terms. The Gospel writer would have each of us as individuals come to know the truth of Christ in our own lives. My sermon on Epiphany Sunday, then, presents the theme of the coming of Christ, the light of the world, first of all as a "hinge moment" for the whole world and then as a "hinge moment" for each of us as individual Christians.

# A SERMON BRIEF

The wise men. Magi. Astrologers from the East. Following a star, seeking the Messiah, the king of the Jews. Walking on the cusp of history—unknowingly. As they travel toward Bethlehem, these wise men have no sense of being part of a momentous, world-changing event. They are on a personal quest, oblivious to the fact that their quest is part of the new thing God is doing in the world. Oblivious to the fact that they are part of a hinge moment in history.

"Hinge moment" is a wonderfully descriptive term for great turning points in the history of the world. Joel Garreau, writing in the *Washington Post* shortly after the attacks on the World Trade Center in September 2001, speaks about hinge moments in history. He suggests they are 1914, 1929, 1945, 1963, 1981, and maybe September 11, 2001. Garreau describes these hinges in history as "pivots on which our lives move from one world to another." He thinks that probably none of us know when we live at a hinge moment in history. It takes time and perspective to be able to define such a moment, much less know you are standing in it. But one thing always happens, he says: "What changes after a hinge is our stories of ourselves."

For Christians, the incarnation, the birth of Jesus Christ, the Word made flesh, is the ultimate hinge moment. The world changes forever with the birth of Jesus Christ; and our stories, our understanding of ourselves, change forever. Christ's birth is not the just "same old, same old," but something new and unique. God discloses Godself. Emmanuel, "God with us." God has come into the world in the person of Jesus Christ, marking the ultimate hinge moment in human history.

*Epiphany* is the Greek word for "coming into the light," "appearance," manifestation." At Epiphany we are celebrating the coming into the light, the appearance of Jesus Christ to the Gentile world.

The Christ event begins with the light of a star whose brilliance leads the Magi to the stable where the baby lies. But this light cannot be confined to a stable or to one people, one tribe, one nation. The birth of Jesus is a hinge moment for all of humankind. Epiphany, the climax of the Christmas season, emphasizes the cosmic and inclusive nature of God's gift of Godself in Jesus Christ.

The church, then, speaks of Epiphany with a capital *E*, as a special day (and season) in the ecclesiastical calendar when we celebrate the coming of Christ as an event in the life of the whole world. But the church also speaks of epiphanies, little *e*, recognizing that throughout the ages people have experienced God individually in different ways and at different times. We may have epiphanies, revelations of God, throughout our lives—if we are as open to the presence of God as were the wise men.

Standing in the middle of Epiphany, the wise men had no sense of the cosmic significance of the event they were right smack in the middle of. They had no sense of that being a hinge moment in the history of the world; but when they knelt before the babe in the manger, they had their own personal epiphanies. Led by the light of the star, they found the little family, and there in the stable they became aware that they were in the presence of the holy. Open, persistent, and eager, they found the Christ Child and fell before him and worshiped. Overwhelmed with joy, they also presented the child with gifts. The light of the world shone on them. And changed them. This was a pivotal moment for each of them. God's grace flooded their lives as the light from the star had flooded their pathway from the East all the way to Bethlehem; and instead of returning to report the location of the baby to the wicked King Herod, they went home by another way. They had been changed.

The story of Epiphany reminds us that we have a long way to go to fulfill the universal and inclusive vision of Epiphany. We—as individuals or as the whole church—have not worked hard enough to ensure that the light of Christ has dispelled the darkness of the world. Nor have we worked hard enough to dissolve the barriers that divide us as people and nations. And finally, neither have most of us personally sought the light of Christ with the same eagerness and persistence as the wise men.

This Sunday we celebrate Epiphany as a hinge moment for the world. May each of you also celebrate this day as a personal epiphany, a moment of your coming afresh to the light of Christ. Does Christ light your way in the world? Are you overwhelmed with joy to be in his presence? What gifts do you have to offer him? Does Christ offer unto you new perspectives, new possibilities, a new way home?

It is a new year, a new beginning, for all of us. This day, Epiphany 2005, celebrate a new beginning in your life. Open your hearts anew to Jesus Christ, the light of the world. Make a New Year's resolution this very day that the light of Christ will shine *in* you, changing and saving you, and that the light of Christ will shine *through* you and be revealed in the world. May this Epiphany Sunday be a little hinge moment for each of you. In the name of Jesus Christ. Amen.

# SUGGESTIONS FOR WORSHIP

## Call to Worship (based on Isaiah 60)

| | |
|---|---|
| LEADER: | Come, let us worship God. |
| **PEOPLE:** | **We come to worship the one true God.** |
| LEADER: | Arise, shine, for your light has come. |
| **PEOPLE:** | **The glory of the Lord has arisen upon us.** |
| LEADER: | Lift up your eyes and look around. |
| **PEOPLE:** | **We lift them up and see God's glory.** |
| LEADER: | Proclaim the praise of the Lord. |
| **PEOPLE:** | **Our hearts are thrilled; we rejoice in the Lord.** |
| ALL: | **Let us worship God.** |

## Prayer of Confession

O gracious and loving God, we come this morning confessing that we have failed to seek you with the eagerness and persistence of the wise men. We have failed to seek you with all our heart, mind, and spirit. Instead of being open to your presence, we have closed you out of our lives. And we have closed out others, failing to hear the cries of the poor and the oppressed. We have shut our eyes, preferring the darkness of the world to the light of Jesus Christ. Forgive us we pray. In the name of Jesus Christ. Amen.

## Assurance of Pardon
## (based on Ephesians 3:1-10)

God, who created all things, has been revealed in Jesus Christ. Through Christ we have access to God; through Christ we receive the gift of saving grace. With boldness and confidence, I declare to you this day, that through the love of God in Jesus Christ, we are forgiven!

# Charge and Benediction

May the light of Christ shine in you and through you, this day and every day.

May the Spirit sustain you always.

May the love of God enfold you forever.

Go in peace—and be a light unto the world.

1. T. S. Eliot, "Burnt Norton" (1935).
2. T. S. Eliot, "Little Gidding" (1942).
3. Joel Garreau, "The Hinges of Opportunity," *The Washington Post* (October 14, 2001), F1.

# Baptism of the Lord

Martha L. Moore-Keish

---

**Isaiah 42:1-9:** God presents the chosen servant to bring justice to the nations.

**Psalm 29:** The voice of God in the storm.

**Acts 10:34-43:** Peter tells Cornelius and other Gentiles the good news of Jesus Christ.

**Matthew 3:13-17:** The baptism of Jesus.

---

## REFLECTIONS

All four Gospels recount Jesus' baptism. Only Matthew, however, has the voice from heaven say, "*This* is my Son, the Beloved . . ." rather than addressing Jesus, "*You* are my Son . . ." Matthew intentionally echoes Isaiah 42:1, the first Servant Song. At the inauguration of Jesus' public ministry, he is cast as the Suffering Servant, who comes to "bring forth justice to the nations." Even as he is called to proclaim justice and release to captives, he starts down the path to Calvary. His baptism is both commissioning to service and acceptance of suffering and death.

Although Matthew identifies Jesus as the Suffering Servant, the identity of the Servant in the context of Second Isaiah is not obvious. Is the Servant an individual, someone of the line of David, or Cyrus? Or, is the Servant the whole people of Israel, called to live "as a covenant to the people, a light to the nations"? It is best not to answer the question too quickly, but to use the ambiguity of individual and collective notions of servanthood.

Isaiah and Matthew together invite meditation on the meaning of baptism. Jesus' baptism was the beginning of his life of suffering servanthood, the first step on the road to his death and resurrection.

Our own baptism joins us to Jesus' death in order that we might be joined to his new life, as individuals and as community. Our baptism also calls us to a life of suffering service.

# A SERMON BRIEF

"On Jordan's stormy banks I stand. . . ." So sang the choir on June 15, 1997, the day my daughter Miriam was baptized. There she was, kicking her bare feet under her white baptismal gown, looking around with solemn two-month-old eyes at the gathered people. What did these words have to do with her? She knew nothing yet of standing on stormy banks—or of standing anywhere at all, for that matter. She knew nothing of wishing for anything more than food, sleep, a face to smile at, and a dry diaper. Isn't this an odd text for infant baptism? Isn't the baptism of infants about God's unconditional love, about God's choosing us before we ever choose anything for ourselves? What does such a baptism have to do with stormy waters or threat of death?

On Jordan's stormy banks Jesus stood facing John. "No," protested John, "I need to be baptized by you, and do you come to me?" "Let it be so now," responded Jesus quietly, "for it is proper for us in this way to fulfill all righteousness." How does this act fulfill righteousness? Wasn't Jesus without sin? Why should he need a baptism of repentance so connected with sin and death?

Yet into the river he went. John plunged him under the waters. And suddenly these were no longer just the murky waters of the Jordan. As Jesus came up gasping, dripping from the river, the heavens opened and he saw the Spirit of God descend like a dove. The Spirit that hovered over the dark waters in the beginning now came to rest on Jesus. In that instant, these ordinary Jordan River waters became the waters of chaos. In that instant, Jesus became the first-born of the new creation. "The voice of the Lord is over the waters," proclaims Psalm 29 today, "the God of glory thunders." And so did the voice from heaven thunder, "This is my Son, the Beloved, with whom I am well pleased."

Water, Spirit, Word. These are the central elements of the first creation in Genesis, and they are the central elements here, as Jesus Christ inaugurates the new creation. When Jesus arose from those waters, and the voice from heaven thundered approval, the earth burst into song:

45

O the transporting, rapturous scene
That rises to my sight!
Sweet fields arrayed in living green,
And rivers of delight. . . .
I am bound for the promised land.

With the coming of Jesus, the promised land rose into view. The former things began to pass away, and the new life was begun.

But all was not sweetness and light on those stormy banks of Jordan. The words from heaven on that day echoed the prophecy of Isaiah regarding a particular servant chosen by God. "This is my Son, the Beloved, with whom I am well pleased," said the voice in Matthew. In Isaiah, God declared, "Here is my servant, whom I uphold, my chosen, in whom my soul delights." In both cases, God chose a particular servant "to bring forth justice to the nations." But also in both cases, God called the chosen one into suffering. The servant in Isaiah was "despised and rejected by others; a man of suffering and acquainted with infirmity" (Isaiah 53:3). Christ, as Suffering Servant, faced temptation, trial, torture, and death. Baptism, the beginning of a life of service, was also the beginning of a life of suffering for the sins of others.

Baptism, our baptism, calls us into a life of suffering for and with others. Baptism does not bring us special privilege. To be baptized in Jesus Christ is to share his calling to suffering service. Not only Jesus, but also we are given as "a light to the nations, to open the eyes of the blind, to bring out the prisoners from the dungeon, from the prison those who sit in darkness." Such a mission is not easy or comfortable. Sister Helen Prejean, portrayed in the movie *Dead Man Walking*, has lived out her baptism by visiting prisoners on Louisiana's death row. She has tried to bring Christ's presence to them, and, remarkably, she has learned to see the face of Christ in the harsh faces and empty eyes of those who "sit in darkness."

Baptism calls us to suffering. Yet baptism, our baptism, also opens our eyes to the new creation in Christ. Sister Helen does not simply sit with those in darkness; nor does she simply bring the light of Christ with her. She sees Jesus Christ already there. This too is our baptismal calling: to see that which others cannot see, to announce that the good news is already here, that the kingdom has already begun. "See, the former things have come to pass," sings Isaiah 42:9, "and new things I now declare; before they spring forth, I tell you of them." Our baptism involves stormy banks, but it also presents "rapturous scenes." In baptism, we plunge into the waters of death, but we also come through to new life, to the promised land.

Why, on Miriam's baptismal day, did we sing about stormy banks and wishful longing for Canaan? Because baptism, even infant baptism, is a dangerous passage. It is the passage from death to life or better, the passage through death to new life in Christ. When we plunge a tiny infant into those waters, we ought to be nervous. This is a death-dealing act. But it is also life-giving. Writer Kathleen Norris presents this tension in a poem about her nephew's baptism. She encourages the poor, sleepy baby to hold on as they pass through hell and renounce the forces of evil. The baby cries out through the waters of baptism as she urges him to hold on, hold on.[1]

Did Miriam, or Norris's nephew, understand what was happening in baptism? Surely not. But the point is not what they understood; the point is they have been called into a community of suffering servanthood, a community that already lives in the new creation begun by Jesus. On this day, we remember Jesus' baptism, and we remember our own baptism. Through water, Spirit, and Word, we renew our commitment to the one who led us through death to life eternal. Delighted, fearlessly, we face Jordan's rolling waves. In the waters of baptism, our lives are both ended and begun, both quenched and launched. Oh, who will come and go with me? We are bound for the promised land. (Following the sermon, the congregation may join in a reaffirmation of the baptismal covenant according to its denominational tradition.)

# SUGGESTIONS FOR WORSHIP

## Call to Worship (Psalm 29:1-4)

| | |
|---|---|
| LEADER: | Ascribe to the Lord, O heavenly beings, |
| **PEOPLE:** | **Ascribe to the Lord glory and strength.** |
| LEADER: | Ascribe to the Lord the glory of his name. |
| **PEOPLE:** | **Worship the Lord in holy splendor.** |
| LEADER: | The voice of the Lord is over the waters, |
| **PEOPLE:** | **The God of glory thunders, the Lord, over mighty waters.** |
| LEADER: | The voice of the Lord is powerful; |
| **PEOPLE:** | **The voice of the Lord is full of majesty.** |

47

# Suggested Hymns

"Crashing Waters at Creation," by Sylvia Dunstan (GIA)
"We Know That Christ Is Raised"
"Out of Deep, Unordered Water"

1. "A. J.'s Passage" in Kathleen Norris, *Little Girls in Church* (Pittsburgh: University of Pittsburgh Press, 1995), 43.

# Ordinary Time 4

### Katie Geneva Cannon

---

**Micah 6:1-8:** "What does the Lord require of you but to do justice, and to love kindness, and to walk humbly with your God?"

**Psalm 15:** Those who do what is right and speak the truth may dwell on God's holy hill.

**1 Corinthians 1:18-31:** The message of the cross is foolishness to those who are perishing, but to those who are being saved it is the power of God.

**Matthew 5:1-12:** The Beatitudes.

---

## REFLECTIONS

The significance of Micah's reproachful chiding in chapter 6 is centered in what Christians in the twenty-first century call orthopraxis, an embodied ethic of right-relating. Micah's prophecy cites faithful living in terms of justice-making action norms rather than ritualistic expectations. Micah investigates and sums up the people's apostasy as wrongheadedness. As people who are partners to the covenant, who have experienced favorable divine acts of power and deliverance, these women, men, and children are guilty on two accounts. First, they are guilty spiritually for allowing fanciful sacrificial offerings to interfere with their social obligations. And, second, they are guilty economically because they curry favors with dominant powerbrokers, and in pecking order fashion pass on their onerous financial burden to the most disinherited in their community. As far as Micah is concerned, this unique relationship between Yahweh and the people of God is threatened with dissolution due to covenantal apostasy. Therefore, if the church is to live as the new covenant, wherein we believe that Jesus Christ reveals the nature and will of God, then our primary mission, according to the prophet Micah, is to keep the covenant alive.

# A SERMON BRIEF

## "Keeping the Covenant Alive"

Being a Christian in today's world is not only difficult, but at times it seems almost impossible. As God-fearing women and men, church-going youth and adults, someone is constantly reminding us, forever challenging us, repetitively teaching us what they think we need to do in order to live as authentic Christians in the twenty-first century.

For instance, we are living in a world wherein increasing isolation is the order of the day. Instead of people of faith coming together in mutual assistance with neighboring communities who are threatened by the HIV/AIDS pandemic, nuclear war, and all kinds of natural disasters, far too many of us close our eyes, stuff our ears, seal our lips, living day in and day out pretending that such death-dealing threats will disappear if we see nothing, hear nothing, and say nothing.

Again, for instance, we are living in a world wherein an upper crust of globalized technocrats, systems analysts, medical scientists, and cyberspace experts loop us with supersonic speed into international statelessness, so much so that the vast majority of us find our social ethics lagging far behind in our inch-by-inch stumbles of daily adaptation.

And, the tendency of so many Christians is to forsake the covenantal mandate that the prophet Micah presents to us in chapter 6. We get so busy multitasking in our sacrificial efforts to carry forth the ministry of the church that others around us tell us we must do, that we forget about the promise we made: "Yes, God will be our God, and we will be God's people." Instead, far too many church folk are guilty of infidelity because we refuse, morning by morning and day by day, to do the three specific things that the Lord requires of us.

The prophet Micah says that doing justice is the first concept we must embrace if we want to keep the covenant alive. Justice is an active virtue demanded by the divine covenant. Justice signifies truth, not merely in the sense of uttering what is right, but more so in doing what is right. Doing justice manifests a highly developed sense of right-relatedness. It is an unconditional reliability in which Christians can have confidence in the integrity of our word and deed.

Thus, Micah uses figurative expressions to enhance our understanding of the rupture between God and people. In order to present adequately an intensive judgment speech against the faithless inhabitants of the land, Micah gives us a legal drama, wherein Yahweh is in the role of prosecutor and judge, and the people who are the partners to the covenant are the accused and sentenced. This oracle summons us to hear the proclamation of our guilt, the evidence of our infidelity, and the legal consequences of our actions.

So, let us ask ourselves, where in our lives do we hear this prophetic indictment of unfulfilled covenant obligations? God, the speaker, is summoning each of us, as the addressee, to answer the soul-searching question that is posed: "[God] has told you, O mortal, what is good; and what does the Lord require of you but to do justice?" The prophet directly confronts the audience with the words of Yahweh, as though Yahweh is delivering the oracle, and our answer is a commanded response. We have a true covenant with God only when we deal justly with one another.

Next, the prophet Micah says that loving-kindness is the second concept we must embrace if we want to keep the covenant alive. Loving-kindness is a virtue that emphasizes authenticity. It denotes genuineness in our attitude that defines and maintains honest and fair dealing in all of our interactions. We love kindness when we responsively do in a given relationship what another can rightly expect according to the norms of the divine commandments, the source of harmonious living among God-fearing people. The essence of loving-kindness is respecting the equality of all people in our daily living.

Like the people's violation in the book of Micah, we too need to investigate where in our lives are we giving undue emphasis to offerings, rituals, and sacrifices, with only a slight attention to life-affirming ethical conduct. The negation of the covenant consists of persecution and victimization of honest people, oppression of the poor, and religious feasts celebrating the material gains wrung from the needy. Where are we repeatedly divorcing religious ritual from moral consideration?

Micah emphasizes that when the covenant is broken, Yahweh's creation suffers the penalties. Micah portrays a loss of life-forces that affect the land, the inhabitants, and every creature. He juxtaposes covenant breaking and disaster. When we are intent on living our lives in death-dealing ways against our neighbors, we not only bring pain and suffering upon them but we bring terrible consequences upon ourselves.

Now, the third thing that the prophet Micah says is that walking humbly with our God is the final concept we must embrace if we want to keep the covenant alive. Micah confronts the people whose fortunes were changing radically, and thus they had fallen victim to the gradual influence of idol worship. Micah preaches that the covenant demands justice, righteous living, and the elimination of elaborate pomp and circumstance in the worship of the true and living God.

As a member of the prophetic movement, Micah was a major contributor to ethical monotheism. Namely, our union with God is not a matter of natural relationship or a magical rite, but as covenant partners, we are required to surrender our life and our will to the care of God. To walk humbly with God implies "reversion" to God that is already revealed and not "conversion" to God as something new. Micah suggests that when we do what the Lord requires of us, that there is physical motion symbolizing our turning back to faithfulness. Those of us who moved away, who might have withdrawn from our covenant with God, when we answer Micah's threefold question in the affirmative; we arrive again at our original point of departure. To walk humbly with our God is to accept God's gift of covenant-love, God's goodness sealed with a promise.

# SUGGESTIONS FOR WORSHIP

## Call to Worship (from Psalm 15)

LEADER:     O Lord, who may abide in your holy tent? Who may dwell on your holy hill?

**PEOPLE:     Those who walk blamelessly, and do what is right,**

LEADER:     Those who speak the truth from their heart and honor those who fear the Lord.

**PEOPLE:     Those who do these things shall never be moved.**

## Call to Confession
## (adapted from 1 Corinthians 1:18-31)

The message about the cross is foolishness to those who are perishing, but to us who are being saved it is the power of God. With faith in God's saving power in Jesus Christ, let us confess our sins.

# Prayer of Confession

Gracious God: We confess that we come before you as those who have pursued the wisdom of the world. We cling to things that are foolish rather than seeking your eternal truths. Forgive us for demanding signs and wisdom. Forgive us for being deluded by the deceptive strength of the world rather than embracing the foolishness—and saving power—of the cross. Inspire us by the example of Jesus Christ, in whom God chose what is weak to shame the strong.

# Assurance of Pardon

God chose what is low and despised in the world, things that are not, to reduce to nothing things that are. God is the source of our life in Christ Jesus, who became for us wisdom from God, and righteousness and sanctification and redemption. Believe this good news, for in Jesus Christ we are forgiven.

# Benediction

Go out into the world in the name of Jesus Christ to do justice, to love kindness, and to walk humbly with our God.

# Transfiguration of the Lord

## Lillian Daniel

**Exodus 24:12-18:** Moses encounters the glory of God on Mount Sinai.

**Psalm 99:** The psalmist extols God's holiness and calls the people to worship at God's holy mountain.

**2 Peter 1:16-21:** Peter and other believers bear witness to the prophetic message of Christ's majesty.

**Matthew 17:1-9:** The transfiguration of Jesus on the mountain in the presence of the disciples.

## REFLECTIONS

Transfiguration Sunday is a time for stretching our holy imaginations. Jesus moves from being an ordinary man climbing a mountain to a shining, angelic figure, floating in the air and suddenly speaking to two great prophets.

To say modern ears are resistant to such a story is an understatement. But postmodern ears are interested in the crossing of boundaries and new ways of seeing. This is an opportunity to reflect on the strangeness of our faith and the mystery of Jesus, who simply will not be confined to a single image, or even to a single moment in time.

So on this Sunday, you might play also with images of God. The confession liturgy uses the traditional imagery of a father God, which strikes me as important on a Sunday in which fatherly love is so poignantly portrayed. But my call to worship takes the kingship imagery of the psalm and replaces it with queenly power, evoking a female image who strikes fear in the hearts of those who do not love justice. Transfiguration Sunday can be a time to transfigure worship as well, so that old things are seen anew.

# A SERMON BRIEF

## "Dazzling and Beloved"

The transfiguration is one of those unexplainable moments that we are almost afraid to touch. How do you grab onto this story in which the disciples were walking up the mountain for a little down time with Jesus, and suddenly Jesus is floating through the sky in glowing white robes, speaking casually to two dead prophets who are also, coincidentally, floating in the air?

When people tell you that Christianity does not relate to their day-to-day lives, this is generally the kind of story they are referring to. This, and the Old Testament dietary laws.

But when it comes to the transfiguration, I disagree. I think this story is as intriguing today as it was back then, because it was as strange back then as it is today. They were as skeptical as we are, no more expecting floating messiahs than we do. The only difference is that they were there experiencing, and we are here reading.

So this Sunday I invite you to enter into the transfiguration with imagination, because imagination is what this story is all about. Not in the sense that it is imaginary, but in the sense that it reminds us that God is greater than what we usually imagine, and that we are greater too.

Just when the disciples thought they knew Jesus, just when they were getting a handle on his mission here on earth, just when they had received the heartbreaking news that Jesus would be killed and then be raised, Jesus surprised them one more time by shooting up into the sky. They never could have imagined that.

Now, Peter was not one for imagination. Peter was the kind of disciple who wanted things nailed down, but not in the sense Jesus had hinted at. Peter wanted to know what the plan was. Generally, when Jesus told him, Peter would argue; but eventually he would come around. Just before this story, when Peter argued with Jesus about his upcoming suffering, Jesus had to get tough with Peter. "Get behind me, Satan," Jesus said. But you had to talk that way to Peter, or he just wouldn't get it.

I often find myself feeling sorry for Peter. Every question he asks Jesus turns out to be wrong. He's always getting smacked down. Why is that? He's a concrete guy in a mystical adventure. Imagination didn't come naturally to Peter, which may be why Jesus had to do outlandish things like the transfiguration.

We love Peter. Peter's the guy here in church who sits in the deacon's meeting listening to all the prayers and sharing, and wondering, "When are we going to get to the details of the communion schedule?" Peter's the woman sitting on the board of trustees listening to all the big dreams about a new building, and wondering, "When are we going to look at the spreadsheets? Because I want to know exactly what this will cost." Peter's the person in church who can put up with a long church service but just wants to know beforehand how long it will go. Just keep me informed. Give me something concrete. Let me know the plan.

So when Jesus was swept up in glorious dazzling robes and appeared next to the prophets, this was not Peter's idea of a good time. James and John may have been swept up in the same mystical delight, but Peter, bless his heart, was thinking about the details. His Lord was floating in the sky. All Peter wanted was a little clarity. Was that too much to ask?

By now, Peter had been parading around the country with this group of mystics long enough to know better than to try to bring Jesus down. By now, Peter was enough in awe of Jesus' power, and enough drawn to it, that he didn't run away screaming, as many of us might have done. In fact, he even threw the mystics a bone, with the acknowledgment "Lord, it is good for us to be here." "But now let me make things a little more concrete," he might have continued. "Let me get out my video camera and record this for the skeptics. Or at least let me build three dwellings around you guys so we have something to remember all this."

It wasn't an outlandish idea. For the Jewish people in that time, place mattered. You built houses of worship on top of places where God was present, and certain places mattered more than others. Peter wanted to mark the spot. But here's the question: was he marking the spot for God, or was he marking the spot like a dog marks territory? Was he claiming this moment for God or for himself? It's as if Peter still thought he could control all this. He still didn't understand that life in Christ meant the end of building dwelling places in which to capture God. For in Christ, we are the ones who are captured, captured in a love in which we dwell, and finding a soft bed that we did not make.

God's voice from the cloud was clearly for Peter, with his Mr. Fix-it ideas of dwelling places and his constant chatter and analysis. "This is my son, the Beloved," God said, "with him I am well pleased." And then, in the tone of voice of a loving but worn-out mom telling the kids in the back of the van to please be quiet because she has something important to say, God adds forcefully, "Listen to him!" And they do. And after that, Jesus returns to the disciples just as they knew him—warm, living, fleshy, and real. It's as if they had to let go of all that was familiar to find comfort in the familiar once again. That change stretched them but did not leave them orphaned.

There's real good news in the transfiguration for people in the church. Very good news indeed. For if you, like Peter, are trapped in the fear that if you don't build it they won't come, think again. We do not build the dwelling places for the Spirit, God does. If you are trapped in the sense that the concrete world is hard and mean, think again. There is always another world, a world of the Holy Spirit in which Jesus and the prophets may be floating just over our heads, if we can open our eyes to see. If you are trapped in old images of God that don't work anymore, images that remind you more of a cruel family member than love, the transfiguration asks us to think again. Jesus shifted himself so many ways for so many people to remind us that we cannot draw or explain God. God draws and explains us. If you yourself are stuck and wondering if it is time for you to change, remember this: if God transfigured Jesus, God can transfigure you as well. The day might come when those who think they know you suddenly see you shining in a whole new light. There you are dazzling but changed, watching the people who are still scurrying around trying to build the next great dwelling place. There you are, new in Christ, knowing that change may be frightening, but change is also God's way of shaping us, of stretching us, of transfiguring us and reminding us that we too are indeed beloved.

When the disciples heard God's voice, they fell to the ground and were overcome by fear. But Jesus came and touched them, saying, "Get up and do not be afraid."

Get up and do not be afraid. For you are dazzling. You are beloved. You too are always being made new. Amen.

# SUGGESTIONS FOR WORSHIP

## Call to Worship (based on Psalm 99)

| | |
|---|---|
| LEADER: | Let the peoples tremble before the queen, our God! |
| **PEOPLE:** | **Holy is she!** |
| LEADER: | She sits enthroned upon the cherubim; |
| **PEOPLE:** | **Let the earth quake.** |

LEADER:      God is great in Zion;
**PEOPLE:     She is exalted over all the peoples.**
LEADER:      Let them praise your great and awesome name.
**PEOPLE:     Holy is she!**
LEADER:      Mighty queen, lover of justice, you have established equity;
**PEOPLE:     You have executed justice and righteousness.**
LEADER:      Holy is she!

# Call to Confession (based on 2 Peter 1)

Jesus received honor and glory from God the Father when that voice was conveyed to him by the Majestic Glory, saying "This is my Son, my Beloved, with whom I am well pleased." Allow us, O God, to hear this same voice come from heaven, as if we were with Jesus on that holy mountain. Hear our silent prayer of confession, as we confess our sin and sadness. Shape our souls and show us that as we repent, we too are your beloved.

(Silent Prayer of Confession)

# Assurance of Pardon
# (based on Matthew 17:5-7)

While Jesus was still speaking, a bright cloud overshadowed them, and from the cloud a voice said, "This is my son, the Beloved, with him I am well pleased. Listen to him!" The disciples were overcome by fear, but Jesus touched them, saying "Get up and do not be afraid." In the power of Christ, from the floor of our faults and foolishness, we get up and we are not afraid.

# Benediction (based on 2 Peter 1:16-21)

Get up and do not be afraid. The God who called Jesus his beloved calls you too. Attend to this word as to a lamp shining in a dark place, until the day dawns and the morning star rises in your hearts. Amen.

# Ash Wednesday

### Tina Cox

---

**Joel 2:1-2, 12-17:** The prophet calls the people to return to the Lord, rending their hearts and not their clothing.

**Psalm 51:1-17:** The psalmist repents and petitions a "clean heart" from God.

**2 Corinthians 5:20b–6:10:** As disciples of Jesus Christ we are called to be reconciled to God and to exhibit qualities of faithfulness.

**Matthew 6:1-6, 16-21:** Jesus' teachings concerning fasting, prayer, and regard for treasure.

---

## REFLECTIONS

Ash Wednesday has become increasingly important in the life of my congregation. I remember the first time we had a service of imposition of the ashes. I had to ask a friend, a Roman Catholic priest, exactly how to prepare ashes! Since that time, I have come to see the non-Sunday Ash Wednesday service as spiritually essential and liturgically significant. Marking the beginning of Lent, it sets the tone for the forty days of preparation by calling us to reflect on our mortality, our sin and shortcomings, and most important, our need for God's grace.

For this Ash Wednesday sermon, I have chosen to focus on the ashes themselves as symbol of death and sin, *and* as an opportunity for new life. I have had the experience of walking over charred fields, our own fields and those in the West following the destruction of great forest fires. All of us have had the experience of seeing the ashes of the World Trade Center after September 11, 2001. I have selected Psalm 51 as the primary text for this sermon. I have also decided to go with the traditional interpretation of Psalm 51 as David's penitential cry to God following his confrontation by Nathan. This psalm is suitable as a preaching text for many occasions, but it is especially suitable as an Ash Wednesday text. My hope is that my congregation will make it their Lenten text, carrying it with them throughout Lent, for it so beautifully and experientially expresses the theme of our need for God's mercy and forgiveness.

What is ultimately decisive in David's situation and ours is not our sinfulness, however, but God's grace. Psalm 51 begins with God, is addressed to God, and ends with God. Only God can make right our relationships with Godself. Only God can turn ashes into new life. Only God can create new hearts within us.

The focus of this Ash Wednesday sermon, therefore, is on calling each of us to begin Lent by standing before God, acknowledging our dependency and our need for forgiveness—as did David. I hope the sermon will open a window through which each of us might be able to see ourselves as smudged with sin and ephemeral in nature. Standing thus before God, we then are overwhelmed by the good news of Jesus Christ.

# A SERMON BRIEF

Several years ago, one dark, cold night our word-burning stove set the woods behind our house on fire. The blaze consumed all of the underbrush and low growing bushes. With daylight, the woods at ground level appeared as charred, blackened ash. Gray and crumbly. Dry and lifeless. No wonder ashes have long been a symbol for death, for the ephemeral nature of life!

In our Judaic-Christian tradition ashes have come to be understood this way—as reminders that "from dust we have come, and to dust we shall return." And by extension, ashes have come to be understood as reminders of the pervasiveness of human sin and the need for confession and repentance.

Today we begin our Lenten journeys with the imposition of the ashes. With the mark on the forehead to remind us of our mortality, we come before God confessing, repenting, and seeking forgiveness— all in preparation for the Easter miracle. Lent, which is formally introduced by Ash Wednesday, is a time for us to set right our relationship with God.

In Psalm 51, our text for this Ash Wednesday service, David is seeking a right relationship with God, or rather he is seeking to repair his relationship with God. Having been confronted by Nathan about his adultery with Bathsheba and his murder of Bathsheba's husband, Uriah, David is forced to admit his sin. He turns to God with confession and contrition and seeks divine forgiveness.

David understands that his life is like an ash heap, that he is completely smudged with sin, that he deserves God's condemnation. He knows he has been consumed by his lust, left a wasteland of a man. Yet, daring to trust the loving and forgiving nature of God, he cries out for forgiveness. "Have mercy on me, O God, according to your unfailing love; according to your great compassion blot out my transgression. Wash away all my iniquity and cleanse me from my sin" (NIV).

Standing before God, creature before Creator, David sincerely, desperately, desires to repair his relationship with the divine: "For I know my transgressions, and my sin is always before me. Against you, you only, have I sinned and done what is evil in your sight." He is not confessing to Nathan, or Bathsheba, or the people of Israel, but to his God.

David's posture before God is a Lenten posture. Acknowledging his sinfulness, he comes before God with a petition for forgiveness, for salvation. It's important to note, though, that his penitential turning toward God was brought about by Nathan's confrontation. David didn't just spontaneously repent of his adultery and murder. Rather, it was the prophet's words that took him to his knees and enabled him to see himself as a sinner before God.

Lent can be for us a similar confrontation. Lent, beginning with Ash Wednesday, confronts us with our sinful natures, forcing us to ask who we are before God. The spiritual disciplines of Lent—prayer and meditation, self-examination and penitence, works of love, Scripture reading, fasting, and the imposition of the ashes—all help prepare us during the forty days before Easter. Beginning in the dry wilderness of our sin, we move toward the cross, acknowledging our need for repentance, and for the mercy and forgiveness proclaimed in the good news of Jesus Christ.

Confession and repentance do not of themselves make right our relationship with God or lead us to salvation. David is redeemed by God's grace, freely given. It is the transforming power of God that redeems David. It is the transforming power of God that redeems us. This Ash Wednesday may we receive the ashes, acknowledging our sinfulness and our dependence on God's grace. May we seek clean hearts and right spirits, knowing that it is only God's amazing grace that restores to us (in David's words) "the joy of our salvation."

After we unintentionally set the woods behind our house on fire, we discovered we were required by law to have the local forest ranger visit the site. After walking about, he turned and said to us: "Next year your mountain laurel will be unusually beautiful!" He knew something we didn't know—that the ashes from the destruction pointed forward to rebirth in the spring.

Out of ashes would come transformation, and renewal, and new life.

The ashes of this day, the first day of Lent, also point forward to the redemptive power of God's grace. The ashes of this day, reminding us of our need for redemption, point forward to the saving power of the cross.

And now, dear friends in Christ, I invite you to come forward for the Imposition of the Ashes.

# SUGGESTIONS FOR WORSHIP

## Call to Worship (based on Joel 2)

LEADER:      Blow the trumpets and sound the alarm; this is the Lord's Day!

PEOPLE:      **We come before the Lord this day with praise and with repentance.**

LEADER:      The Lord is gracious and merciful, slow to anger and abounding in steadfast love.

PEOPLE:      **We the Lord's people gather in solemn assembly.**

LEADER:      Even now, the Lord says: Return to me with all your heart.

PEOPLE:      **We return to the Lord.**

ALL:      **Let us worship God.**

## Confession of Sin

Loving and forgiving God, on this Ash Wednesday, we confess before you alone our sins and shortcomings. You have said that you desire that we come to you in secret to unburden our souls, and so we have come. Hear now our secret, private confessions. (Silent confession)

As we begin our Lenten journeys, O God, we begin by acknowledging our need for your mercy. Blot out our transgressions, wash us thoroughly, cleanse us of our sin. Prepare us for the miracle of Easter. This we ask in the name of Jesus Christ. Amen.

# Assurance of Pardon

When we, like David, sincerely confess our sins before God, God receives and restores us. God creates clean hearts and right spirits within us. Friends, believe the good news through the love of God in Jesus Christ; we are forgiven!

# Charge and Benediction

Go forth from here this Ash Wednesday knowing that the ashes of this day point forward to the redemptive power of the Resurrection. And may God's grace flow over you, drawing you ever more to Jesus Christ, and filling you ever more with the Holy Spirit. Go and begin your Lenten journeys.

# First Sunday in Lent

Stacey Simpson Duke

---

**Genesis 2:15-17; 3:1-7:** The story of sin and punishment in the garden of Eden.

**Psalm 32:** The psalmist sings of the assurance of God's forgiveness.

**Romans 5:12-19:** Sin came into the world through Adam but grace came through Jesus Christ.

**Matthew 4:1-11:** The temptation of Jesus.

---

## REFLECTIONS

Regarding the story of the Fall in Genesis, Phyllis Trible says, "A happy ending to the story is impossible; only the aftermath of disaster remains."[1] Where does that leave the preacher? How do we preach good news from a text fundamentally about human disobedience and sin?

Moreover, how do we preach such a text when historically readers have placed so much of that disobedience and sin squarely on the shoulders of Eve? How does the preacher resist and even refute centuries of misogynistic interpretation, while at the same time preach a sermon and not a diatribe?

For me, the best place to start is with acknowledging the pain and shame that traditional interpretation of this text has perpetuated. To do that, the whole of the text must be considered. The lectionary arbitrarily ends the story with verse 7. For preaching, I believe all of chapter 3 must be taken into account. It will certainly be in the minds of most listeners; the preacher might as well make it explicit.

As a preacher, I want to find some word beyond merely acknowledging "the aftermath of disaster." Certain questions occur to me as potentially fruitful: What does this story teach us about trust and mistrust? Why do we call this story "The Fall?" When our eyes are opened, what do we see? And, what can we learn from this story that might help us toward keeping a holy Lent?

# A SERMON BRIEF

Barbara Kingsolver's book *The Poisonwood Bible* tells the story of a fierce evangelical missionary from the viewpoint of his wife and four daughters. Throughout the novel, the missionary's actions tilt progressively toward emotional and spiritual abuse of his family. Meanwhile, each of the females struggles to deal with his domination.

At one point, his wife tries to explain why she let her husband treat her and their daughters the way he did:

> This is not a new story: . . . I'd come to believe that God was on his side. . . . I feared him more than it's possible to fear a mere man. Feared Him, loved Him, served Him, clamped my hands over my ears to stop His words that rang in my head even when He was far away, or sleeping. In the depths of my sleepless nights I would turn to the Bible for comfort, only to find myself regaled yet again. *Unto the woman God said: I will greatly multiply thy sorrow and thy conception, in sorrow thou shalt bring forth children; and thy desire shall be to thy husband, and he shall rule over thee.*
> Oh, mercy. If it catches you in the wrong frame of mind, the King James Bible can make you want to drink poison in no uncertain terms.[2]

I know what she means—and it's not just the King James Version, either. Some of the stories in Scripture are downright disturbing. More disturbing still is how we've used them against each other. Some of our cruelest behaviors are done in the name of God and Scripture.

When I was thirteen, my father told me about a front-page article in the newspaper. The Southern Baptist Convention had passed a resolution stating that women were not to preach or serve in any position of "pastoral authority." The resolution included several Bible verses and one chilling statement: "because women are responsible for the Edenic Fall. . . ."

I laughed, assuming my dad had made it up. My family's own Southern Baptist church—into which I had just been baptized—had never made such statements about women. Sure, I had never heard a woman preach, had never seen a woman pastor, had never heard anyone say that a woman *could pastor,* but I had not yet heard anyone say she *couldn't.* At age thirteen I had no idea yet that I was being called into pastoral ministry, but I knew that something almost like a crime had just been committed against me by my own denomination.

What I didn't realize was that the problem goes far beyond the misogynist impulses of the SBC. The history of how this story has been used to keep women in their place is long and disgraceful.[3]

The worst news for women, though, comes not through myopic interpretation, but from the text itself. The punishment for the sin is particularly brutal for women: painful childbirth, yet a desire for men, who will dominate them. So often these words have been heard as a decree: this is how God ordained gender relations to be. Yet clearly this is not the original divine intention. Only through human disobedience does God's good creation get corrupted. In fact, one of the main truths this story tells is this: everything that's wrong with us came as a consequence of sin rather than divine intention.

So how did this mess happen? We are each made in the beautiful image of God; and in the very beginning God looked at us, smiled, and said, "Yes, this is good. This is very good." But all we have to do is look around us to see that things aren't so good, and we are not so very good. What happened to all that blessed goodness?

The Bible answers with a story. God planted a garden in Eden, in the east, and there he put the man and woman he had made. "You may freely eat of every tree of the garden," God told them. "But of the tree of the knowledge of good and evil you shall not eat, for in the day that you eat of it you shall die" (Genesis 2:16-17).

"You will not die," the serpent hisses (Genesis 3:4). And this is how it begins. What was once a given—trust in God's goodness—is now treated as naïveté.

What happened when they took the fruit and ate? At that precise moment, they reached beyond the boundary set by God. They decided that there was something better than living within the limits set by God, something better than trusting and enjoying the goodness of God—so they reached for knowledge and power over the mysteries that once were known only by God.

This is how the fall happens—and this is how we keep falling. Not in the decision to disobey. Not in the decision to do evil. But in the mistrust of God's goodness, in the reaching beyond God's limits to conquer mystery, and in the determination to take our lives into our own hands.

The snake was right about what would happen once the man and woman took what didn't belong to them. Their eyes were opened. What they saw was their own nakedness and shame. And we, like them, have seen our shame. We are all "fallen," which is to say that we aren't nearly what we were meant to be and we know it.

The serpent was right about another thing, too—they didn't die. They lived on long past their mistake. Long enough to regret it. Long enough to blame each other for their problems. Long enough to know that there are many kinds of dying.

This is where we start our Lenten journey. East of paradise. No way back. The only way now is forward—toward the cross. The thing to do with our open eyes at this point is to look long and hard, to see who we are and how we've fallen short. Denial about our condition has never made it better. Once we've really seen what's in our hearts, we can see how clearly we need the One who came to save us.

In the beginning, there was a tree. On that tree, there was a tempter. What he offered was knowledge. He said, "Take it. Eat it."

A long time passed. There was another tree. On that tree, hung one who was tempted but did not sin. What *he* offered was life. He said, "This is my body, given for you. Take. Eat." And through his self-sacrificing love, he gave us the one thing we could not take for ourselves. New life. New hearts. Not what we grasped for, but what we needed most of all.

# SUGGESTIONS FOR WORSHIP

## Call to Worship (based on Matthew 4:1-11)

LEADER:     In the midst of his temptation, Jesus taught us how to survive our own wilderness;

PEOPLE:     **And so we pray and live his words.**

LEADER:     "One does not live by bread alone, but by every word that comes from the mouth of God."

PEOPLE:     **By the words of God's mouth, we have been brought to life and new life.**

LEADER:     "Do not put the Lord your God to the test."

PEOPLE:     **In the midst of trials and tribulations, we renew our trust in God.**

LEADER:     "Worship the Lord your God and serve only him."

PEOPLE:     **We have come to worship and to serve.**

ALL:     **Let us worship the Lord our God—and live.**

# Prayer of Confession

God of healing and wholeness, we confess that we have fallen and even broken. We have too often listened to the lies of the world and doubted your goodness and wisdom. We have been hurt by the stories we have been told about you and about ourselves, and we have perpetuated those stories and that hurt. We have denied your Spirit in ourselves, in others, and in all creation. As we begin our journey into Lent, help us to come to a deeper recognition of our humanity and a firmer embrace of your redemption. Lord, have mercy.

# Assurance of Pardon

In Jesus, God has entered the garden of this world in order to find us and redeem us. In Christ, we are made whole and new. In the name of Jesus Christ, we are forgiven. Thanks be to God! Amen.

# Benediction

And now may the love of God the Creator undergird us, may the peace of Jesus Christ dwell in us, and may the power of the Holy Spirit move through us.

Go in grace, to pray, to love, and to live a new life. Amen.

1. Phyllis Trible, *God and the Rhetoric of Sexuality* (Philadelphia: Fortress Press, 1978), 132.
2. Barbara Kingsolver, *The Poisonwood Bible* (New York: HarperFlamingo, 1998), 192.
3. For example, in Milton's retelling of the Genesis story, he practically absolves Adam of all responsibility, making it seem that Eve stood at the tree alone, chatting with the snake and picking fruit. Augustine, likewise, casts Eve as temptress and bringer of original sin.

# Second Sunday in Lent

### M. Jan Holton

---

**Genesis 12:1-4a**: God promises to make Abram's descendants a great nation.

**Psalm 121**: The psalmist declares that our help "comes from the Lord who made heaven and earth."

**Romans 4:1-5, 13-17**: Abraham is held up as an example of God's promise realized through faith.

**John 3:1-17**: Nicodemus visits Jesus at night and learns the way to eternal life.

---

## REFLECTIONS

Nicodemus's struggle reflects the tension between two moments of creation, the physical and the spiritual. Jesus is preparing his visitor for the task of discipleship by giving him the tools he, and we, will need to navigate the world as new creatures born of the Spirit. First, we discover the *gifted-ness* of choosing a life in Christ. Being born from above is pure gift. Receiving Christ is a choice. Together the gift and the choice bring new life. Second, Jesus is clear that one cannot even recognize the kingdom of God unless she or he is born of the Spirit. Once born again, we are given new eyes through which we can see the world with *kingdom potential*. Finally comes the sum of all that Jesus says: the Son of Man must be lifted up. The symbol of the cross becomes that which both gives us respite *from* the broken world and simultaneously propels us *into* it.

Nicodemus remains a shadow figure throughout the Gospel of John. He appears only briefly and emerges quietly from the periphery of the story. Even so the placement of these appearances should not be overlooked and are particularly fitting when we consider them in the context of the Lenten season. In chapter 7 we find Nicodemus trying to muster enough courage to defend Jesus against the other Pharisees who were calling for his arrest. Finally, Nicodemus steps forward with Joseph of Arimathea to remove Jesus' body from the cross in preparation for burial. While ultimately it is left to the reader to discern what was the impact upon Nicodemus of this encounter with Jesus, one should not dismiss this journey through the night as that of a fool. Perhaps it is just this kind of struggling, doubtful timidity that reflects the messiness of our own faith journeys.

# A SERMON BRIEF

## "Standing in the Shadow of the Cross"

Who is this man Nicodemus? I have often thought of him as a rather dull-witted man best known to us for his inability to grasp even the simplest elements of the gospel message. With the passage of time I have come to believe that he deserves a closer look. This passage tells us a few things about Nicodemus, though some of them only implicitly. This is not just anyone sneaking through the night to see Jesus. In the eyes of many in his community he is the wisest among the wise. I can imagine those who would travel near and far to seek *his* counsel. How would it appear if anyone should see Nicodemus sneaking under the cloak of night to sit at the feet of this renegade teacher? Could it be that Nicodemus comes to Jesus asking these questions not because he is dull of mind but rather because he is a wise man able to discern that somewhere in Jesus' message is the gift of life for which he would risk everything?

As I envision Nicodemus on that night, a seminary professor I once had comes to mind. Perhaps somewhere along the road you too have had a teacher like him. He is a brilliant man. But his wisdom comes, I think, not so much from all that he knows (which is a lot) but from his willingness to admit what he does *not* know. I tried to imagine him in Nicodemus's shoes, sneaking through the night to ask questions of this great teacher—willing even to risk his reputation in order to understand.

What is Nicodemus missing? What is the key that would give Nicodemus that aha! moment of clarity? He is, after all, a faithful man who understands that God is the God of the heavens and the earth. He understands that this is the "God which is your shade at your right hand" (Psalm 121:5b), the God of grace, of whom the psalmist speaks so longingly. What's missing?

Jesus has told Nicodemus—and us—several very important things about what it means to be born again into the Spirit of God. First, we cannot be born anew by ourselves. In this do-it-yourself world, we cannot just decide to take matters into our own hands. No, only by God's love and grace are we born anew. It is a gift. There is nothing that we can do to earn it. However, neither is it a gift that is forced upon us. Always, it is our *choice* whether to receive God's blessing or to reject it.

To be born of the spirit means to see the world with a new clarity. Recently I discovered, with the help of my new ophthalmologist, that the contact lenses I have been wearing for several years were ill-fitted to my eyes. The result? The corneas had literally become warped and my vision unstable. For two weeks I let my eyes rest. As each day passed, my corneas began to settle back into their natural shape. And, with every day my vision became more blurred, everything distorted. By week's end, I could no longer drive at night, reading was very difficult, and discerning anything at a distance was nearly impossible. I began to feel the fear of how little I could see without even my ill-fitted lenses to rely on. Finally, I was fitted with a new pair of glasses. I was quite a sight! One moment I was practically swooning from the strength of the lenses, the next moment I was almost giggling with joy at all that I could see. And how clear everything became! I started to notice things, small things, that I had never seen before, even in my own home. A hidden color in a painting emerged with a sudden brilliance. The letters in the book I had been reading became sharp and clear—just inviting me to read them! How clearly I came now to see the face of my father, who passed away not long ago, in the photo that sits in view of my favorite chair. I have been surprised by the joy of it all.

To be born again gives us those special lenses that invite us to see the world in a special way. It becomes very hard not to see the things we so easily overlooked before. The *invisible* people in our community and world—the poor, the lonely, the sick, the oppressed—take on a sudden brilliance to our eyes. And yet somehow even when we see the raw ugliness around us, we are able, still, not only to find hope but to be filled by it. When we can see the kingdom of God in our midst, we see the world with the eyes that demand justice and peace and accept nothing less. These are the eyes that can only be born from above.

To be born of the Spirit, Jesus tells us, draws our vision upward toward the cross. When we are finally willing to stand in the shadow of the cross, looking up toward the crucified Christ, then we will stand fully in the presence of what it is to be born as *new* creatures, free from the burdens of our past failures and inadequacies. Though we stand in a shadow of suffering, witnessed by the pain and death of Christ, it is also a place where the cool shade of God's grace gives us refuge. This is the very shade the psalmist promises us: "The LORD is your keeper; the LORD is your shade at your right hand. The sun shall not strike you by day, nor the moon by night" (Psalm 121:5-6).

If we think that this shade is a leisurely spot that allows us to sit in comfort while the rest of the world passes us by, we have another thought coming. The psalmist understands shade in a very different way than do we. It is not the vast shade of the grand oaks and maples under which we sit in our backyards. No, for a desert dweller there is no such plentiful shade. In the heat of the desert sun, shade, even a small parcel of it, can be life-saving and life-giving. It is so scarce that to find it when one is in need is nothing short of God's hand at work. Even so, the shade never stays in the same place for very long. Always it is moving. And so it is with us—we must be moving and never turning from the brokenness of the world. The shade of the cross is that place where we come for respite, to relieve our weary selves, even if just for a few moments, but always we must move again into the world.

What is missing for Nicodemus in this story is the shade of the cross. Does Nicodemus ever get it? Of this we cannot be certain. But when last we see Nicodemus in the Gospel of John he stands with Joseph of Arimathea at the foot of the cross, gently removing the broken body of Christ and laying him in the tomb. Perhaps, just perhaps, in a brief moment he may have glanced up as he stood in the shadow of the cross and at last understood the depth of its meaning.

# SUGGESTIONS FOR WORSHIP

## Opening Prayer (based on Genesis 12:1-4*a*)

You sent Abraham from the comfort of his people to the strangeness of a new land.

So we have journeyed from many places to gather before you this day.

To him you gave your promise of greatness and blessing for all generations to come.

Give to us, O God, the faith of Abraham, so that we too may share in that promise.

Open our hearts this day, O God, as we prepare to worship you.
Bless this time with your presence.

Receive now, O God, the joys and sorrows of our hearts and the songs of our spirit that we lift up to you this day in praise and worship. Amen.

# Litany of Response

ONE:    O Lord, grant us courage to accept, again and again, your invitation to new life.

ALL:    **Give us the eyes of one born into the Spirit so that we may see both the blessings and sorrows of your children in the world.**

ONE:    As we move toward the cross during this Lenten time, make us mindful of all that it demands of us as disciples.

ALL:    **Let us remember, too, the joy of your love that sent your Son into the world.**

ONE:    Give us strength, Lord, to face the horror of the cross.

ALL:    **Even so, Lord, teach us to seek the cross when we are weary, for in its shadow we find respite from our heavy burden.**

ONE:    But nudge us gently if we tarry there too long or believe that our work is done.

ALL:    **Each day of our journey, Lord, may we be your disciples born of the Spirit and awash with your love. Amen.**

# Third Sunday in Lent

Barbara J. MacHaffie

---

**Exodus 17:1-7:** After the Israelites complained to Moses of their thirst, God answered Moses' plea and made water flow from a rock.

**Psalm 95:** The psalmist praises the Lord as "the rock of our salvation."

**Romans 5:1-11:** Because we are justified by our faith in Jesus Christ, as Paul reminds the Romans, we enjoy the benefits of reconciliation with God.

**John 4:5-42:** A Samaritan woman fulfills Jesus' request for a drink at the well and discovers "living water."

---

## REFLECTIONS

As feminist scholars have revisioned this story of the Samaritan woman at the well, the text has acquired new significance and vitality for many Christians. Such scholars have valued this text as a classic example of the countercultural attitudes of Jesus toward women. He is willing to accept a drink from a woman regarded by his own people as unclean from birth. He converses with her on theological issues despite rabbinic opinion that a Jewish male should not talk to women in public. And he sends this woman as a witness to his messiahship in opposition to a culture that distrusted the testimony of women in courts of law. This Samaritan woman thus becomes, like many women in John's Gospel, a model disciple.

Yet even many of the revisionists assume that the story is primarily about the sexual morality of the Samaritan woman. She has had five husbands and the man she now has is not her husband. Bonnie Thurston, in her book *Women in the New Testament,* provides us with a different perspective on this text.[1] Could this woman, for example, have been the victim of repeated levirate marriages that required the closest male relative of each of her deceased husbands to marry her and reclaim his relative's "property"? Was she the victim of a culture in which a man could divorce his wife for trivial reasons such as burning a meal? Was she compelled to remarry time after time in order to ensure a livelihood for herself and thus survival?

But Thurston continues to revision this text by raising the question of whether Jesus is even asking about the woman's husbands. She suggests that when the Aramaic term *ba'al,* which means either husband or false god, was translated into Greek, the term for husband was normally used. But in some texts, the notion of "false god" might be more accurate. The passage, therefore, may not be about a procession of men in this woman's life but about her own flitting from religion to religion. She lived in an empire that certainly offered an astonishing array of religious choices, and the Romans were always ready to absorb another religion as long as it did not threaten civil order. Also, the conversation she has with Jesus is logical and well-informed. The only jarring note is verse 20 when she talks about places of worship, and this comment makes sense if they are discussing her role as a religious seeker. Perhaps, then, she is shopping for faith, trying to make a good choice. In this encounter, however, she becomes the one who is chosen, chosen for conversation, redemption, and discipleship.

# A SERMON BRIEF

## "Savvy Shopping at the Well"

Despite recent experiences of economic downturn and recession, America in the new millennium has continued to enjoy a period of unprecedented prosperity. We consume a quantity and range of material goods that would have been astonishing even a few decades ago. While a Lexus and a "McMansion" may still be possible only for those with high incomes, I see ordinary neighbors around me with cell phones and Palm Pilots and regular deliveries from QVC, the shopping channel. It appears that consumption has become not only a way of life, but a reason for living.

The economic prosperity of recent years is the latest manifestation of a general rise in material wealth that began after the Second World War. And this prosperity has been driven by the ability of the marketplace to give people what they want. We as consumers have been placed on pedestals by companies eager to satisfy our every desire. We choose from an almost endless array of goods on the shelf as Burger King cries in our ears, "Have it your way!"

While few of us can honestly say that we do not value choice in what and how much we consume, choice can be treacherous. Our role as consumers has come to shape our identity as human beings, and we readily cast the eye of the savvy shopper over important aspects of our lives. We change long-distance phone carriers and brokers; we move from school to school, church to church, and relationship to relationship. Commitments therefore seem less urgent. Not long ago I read a cautionary article on consumer culture in which the author observed that life has become a kind of supermarket in which people choose whatever makes them happy. They can choose divorce if their marriage no longer pleases them, drugs if they want to change their mood, and surgery if their appearance has grown old and worn. Many college students are academic nomads, leaving one institution after a short time because they didn't make the team or didn't like an instructor. Scholars often describe the past couple of decades in American religion as a time of unrestrained and unprecedented experimentation. People ignore previous attachments to dogma and denomination as they try to find a group that meets their needs. Teenaged Josie in Gail Godwin's novel *Evensong* even regards prayer as merchandise, saying that she doesn't like the Lord's Prayer, and asking the Reverend Margaret Gower, "What else have you got?"[2]

Living in a culture that panders to the consumer also makes us believe that we can engineer a perfect life—if we make the right choices. Anyone who watches television in our culture is barraged with messages that say, "If you read the right newspaper, you can create a startup company which will bring you unimaginable wealth," or "If you choose the right paint roller, your living room can be painted in less than an hour." The consequence of wrong choices, of course, is disaster; and plenty of advertisers also trade on this fear. Finally, there is danger in an approach to life that says, "I am the customer, and my voice is really the only one that matters." The other important voices in our lives—voices of the community and voices from the past—are somehow lost.

New Testament scholar Bonnie Thurston's interpretation of the story of the woman at the well makes me think that this Samaritan woman might have fit right into our savvy shopper culture. Was she looking for a perfect life by finding the perfect religion? Was she listening only to the voices of her own needs and desires? Was she afraid of commitment? The astonishing thing about this story is that Jesus chooses her; he chooses her for conversation and redemption and discipleship. And here is a reminder that the good news of the gospel is not about choosing but about being chosen—being chosen for God's love and forgiveness and amazing grace simply by virtue of our humanity. The gospel in a sense turns the way of the world— which makes consumer choice sacred—on its head. We love because God first loved us. And this good news is rooted in a grand and profound tradition that emphatically stated that the people of Israel were chosen for covenant and community. Indeed, says God, the whole earth is mine, but you shall be for me a priestly kingdom.

The Samaritan woman, then, might teach us that while choice is good, we are redeemed from its dangers in our lives of faith. The voices of others, past and present, become important. We are called to commitment in response to being chosen. And, above all, we begin to experience life made perfect because it is centered on God who first loved us and chose us in Christ Jesus.

# SUGGESTIONS FOR WORSHIP

## Call to Worship (Psalm 95:6-7)

LEADER:     O come, let us worship and bow down, let us kneel before the Lord our Maker!

PEOPLE:     **For the Lord is our God, and we are the people of God's pasture, and the sheep of God's hand.**

## Prayer of Confession

Gracious God, who has chosen all creation for love and redemption, forgive our restless pursuit of self-satisfaction. Forgive our delusion that what we buy and what we achieve can bring us lasting peace. Forgive our readiness to abandon commitments when we are the least bit inconvenienced. And forgive us when we listen only to the voice of our own needs. We forget that we are part of a community, past and present, that has much to teach us. Remind us that what we truly need has already been supplied in abundance through your generous grace. Amen.

# Assurance of Pardon (from Romans 5)

Therefore, since we are justified by faith, we have peace with God through our Lord Jesus Christ, through whom we have obtained access to this grace in which we stand. Friends, believe the good news of the gospel: in Jesus Christ we are forgiven.

# Benediction

Go into the world in peace, seeking commitment and community. And go in the assurance that we love because God first loved us. Amen.

1. Bonnie Thurston, *Women in the New Testament: Questions and Commentary* (New York: Crossroad, 1998).
2. Gail Godwin, *Evensong* (New York: Ballentine Books, 1999), 75.

# Fourth Sunday in Lent

## Tracy Hartman

---

**1 Samuel 16:1-13:** Samuel meets the young man David and recognizes him as the one chosen for anointing by the Lord.

**Psalm 23:** The psalmist calls the Lord "shepherd" and wants for nothing.

**Ephesians 5:8-14:** The Ephesians are called to live as "children of light."

**John 9:1-41:** Jesus heals a man born blind and faces challenges from the Pharisees.

---

## REFLECTIONS

Psalm 23 is so familiar that it is difficult to preach. Even most nonchurched folk can quote all or part of the psalm, and in their minds it is usually associated with funerals. J. Clinton McCann, Jr., asserts that although this psalm is an important one for funerals, it is perhaps even more appropriately used as a psalm about living. "For it puts daily activities, such as eating, drinking, and seeking security, in a radically God-centered perspective that challenges our usual way of thinking."[1] Here is a fresh Lenten word for us.

In our individualistic society, most people have developed attitudes of self-reliance and self-trust. They seek security and fulfillment in wealth and stature. In this context, the Twenty-third psalm is both a call to individual rest and an invitation to join with others as members of God's family.

In the ancient Near East, the image of shepherd was used as a metaphor for the king who was to support, guide, and protect the people. We are called to put our trust in this shepherd God who is deemed worthy and faithful of our trust. James Mays points out that

79

trust is not just a matter of mood. Strength must be found, a way walked, and harm and evil must be overcome even though enemies persist. The foundations of this type of trust in Psalm 23 are prayer, a spirit of thanksgiving for one's salvation, and connection with Israel's testimony to its salvation in the Exodus.[2] This context kept early readers of this psalm from interpreting it in a way that was too individualistic and subjective.

Psalm 23 can be connected to the Lord's Supper in that both invite us to live under God's rule and in solidarity with all God's children. This is a radical affirmation of faith that transforms life and the world, and it is a fitting message for the Lenten season.

# A SERMON BRIEF

If you're like me, the peaceful images in the Twenty-third psalm don't sound much like reality. There is green grass in my yard, and right now it needs to be mowed. There are still waters in our garden pond, along with a winter's worth of leaves and muck that need to be cleaned out. Our table will only be laden with food after we get home from church and prepare it. In fact, our lives are often just the opposite of this psalm. See if you relate more to this description of life:

> The clock is my dictator, I shall not rest.
> It makes me lie down only when exhausted.
> It leads me to deep depression.
> It hounds my soul.
> It leads me in circles of frenzy for activity's sake.
> Even though I run frantically from task to task,
> I will never get it all done
> For my "ideal" is with me.
> Deadlines and my need for approval, they drive me.
> They demand performance from me, beyond the limits of my schedule.
> They anoint my head with migraines.
> My in-basket overflows.
> Surely fatigue and time pressure shall follow me all the days of my life,
> And I will dwell in the bonds of frustration forever.[3]

Does this sound all too familiar? How have we let our lives get so far out of hand? Some of us have listened to the voices around us, urging us to drive ourselves to continually work harder so that we can acquire more. Others of us are driven by a need for approval. The more diligently we work, the more we accomplish, and the more we are rewarded with the praise and commendations we crave. Still others of us drive ourselves relentlessly, knowing that if we slow down and get quiet, our private demons will haunt us yet again. We long for the inner peace and tranquillity that we hear about in the psalm, but we fear how we will have to change to achieve such a state. During this season of Lent, when we are called to reflect on our lives individually and corporately, we realize that the way we are living falls far short of God's best intentions for us.

But how do we achieve such a life, we ask? Sometimes it seems that the only way to get out of the rat race is to move to an isolated cabin in the mountains or to become a monk or a nun and hole up in a convent. These are not realistic solutions for most of us. And they are not our real answers. The real answer lies in learning to cultivate a quieter and more contemplative lifestyle in the midst of the lives that we live. The real answer lies in transferring our trust from ourselves to God, who truly loves us and desires to meet our basic needs.

The key in helping us accomplish this transfer of trust is to gain a different perspective. In the psalm we learn that God is relentlessly pursuing us with goodness and mercy and an invitation to peace and restoration. Instead of looking over our shoulders at deadlines and pressures and the faces that haunt our pasts, we are called to look back and see the face of a loving God who walks with us through our deepest waters and offers us peace and rest and banqueting in the midst of our enemies and trials.

In the time when this psalm was written, the image of shepherd was used as a metaphor for the king. In that day, it was the king's responsibility to protect and provide for the people. Often they did not, just as our rulers and governments do not provide for us today. However, this psalm powerfully reminds us that God is a faithful provider and protector, and that we are called to put our trust in God's loving care.

Finally, this psalm implicitly reminds us that we are not alone in our journeys. The Israelites, who first sang this song in worship, knew the history of God's saving work among them. They recalled these stories often as they gathered for worship and prayer. They knew that the invitation in this psalm, as personal as it sounds, was an invitation to live under God's rule in solidarity with all of God's children. Their response was a radical affirmation of a faith that transforms our lives and the world around us.

Cleland McAfee learned firsthand what it meant to trust in God in the midst of the difficult circumstances of his life. As a pastor in Chicago in 1901, he was stunned to receive the news that his two beloved nieces had died from diphtheria. Turning to God and the Scriptures in his grief, he found comfort, shelter, and peace. During this time, he composed a song to comfort himself and his family. On the day of the funerals, he stood with his choir outside the quarantined home of his brother and sang with assurance the comforting words of the hymn we know as "There Is a Place of Quiet Rest, Near to the Heart of God."

In the midst of the turmoil of our lives this Lenten season, may we slow down enough that God's offer of goodness and mercy may overtake us and wash over us and restore us to peace and rest. May we pause long enough to be reminded of God's faithfulness to us in the past, and may we join with our brothers and sisters in learning to trust in Jesus, our Good Shepherd, to provide for our needs. Through this journey, may we catch a glimpse of the kingdom of God on earth and join together in making it a transforming reality in our midst. In quietness and peace may we draw near to the heart of God. Amen.

# SUGGESTIONS FOR WORSHIP

## Call to Worship

LEADER: The Lord is our shepherd, we shall not want.
**PEOPLE: He makes us lie down in green pastures;**
LEADER: He leads us beside still waters;
**PEOPLE: He restores our souls.**
LEADER: Let us worship the Lord.

## Benediction

Go out into the world in the knowledge and care of the Lord who is our shepherd, who prepares a table of abundance for us even amidst our enemies, who fills our cups with goodness until they overflow. And may we dwell in the house of the Lord our whole life long.

1. J. Clinton McCann, *Psalms, New Interpreters Bible,* vol. 4 (Nashville: Abingdon Press, 1996), 767.
2. James L. Mays, *Psalms, Interpretation Commentary* (Louisville: John Knox Press, 1994), 118.
3. "Psalm 23, Antithesis," by Marcia K. Hornok. Used by permission.

# Fifth Sunday in Lent

### Donna Hopkins Britt

---

**Ezekiel 37:1-14:** Ezekiel receives a vision of the valley of dry bones.

**Psalm 130:** The psalmist cries "out of the depths" to the Lord and awaits God's redemption.

**Romans 8:6-11:** A description of life in the Spirit.

**John 11:1-45:** The story of the death and raising of Lazarus.

---

## REFLECTIONS

As we approach Passion Week and Jerusalem, we become more aware of our brokenness. We become more aware that we put Jesus on the torturous cross. We find it easier to go along with the crowd than to stand against it; we tend to accept the accepted and marginalize the marginalized; we cross to the other side of the road when someone is in need; we doubt that Lazarus or others can be revived or healed.

As broken people in our disconnected and fragmented world, Ezekiel's story of inviting God to re-create life for dry bones offers hope that even when we are feeling spiritually dry, or tempted, or weak, or disconnected, God, through people, can draw us, also, back to wholeness.

## A SERMON BRIEF

### "Agents of Resurrection"

Now the city picks up our recyclables from a bin on the street, but we used to have to take them to the recycling center. It was most fun when I had glass spaghetti jars or jelly jars to throw into the bin of glass. Perhaps it's similar to the release some people get out of hitting a tennis ball when they're stressed; for me, the sound of glass shattering and clinking as it settled into the crevices created by other jars and bottles was a thrill in this safe place. Lots of things look fun but are not safe to do: playing with the mercury from a broken thermometer, straddling your car down the yellow line in the middle of the highway, or throwing a glass bottle against a wall to watch it break.

The glass never can be put back together as it was. Perhaps in the recycling process a few molecules might end up together, but the original glass jar, like Humpty Dumpty, will never be the same. Sometimes we feel as broken as the jars in that recycle bin, as if we'll never be whole again.

The opposite is true in the story from Ezekiel. Whether in a vision or in reality, Ezekiel is looking across a desolate valley full of dry, bleached bones. As the Lord leads Ezekiel all around them, there appears to be no sign of life, paralleling this point in the history of the Jewish people. They were in exile, as if in a valley of death. Their temple in Jerusalem had been destroyed; they had been deported to Babylon, and while reports say that life wasn't so bad over there, it wasn't home. It felt foreign and dry and desolate.

The Lord asks Ezekiel, "Mortal, can these bones live?" His answer is uncertain: "O Lord GOD, you know" (v. 3).

In other words, "Lord, is this a trick question?" Sometimes we do wonder what God is up to when something is going on that we don't understand. Ezekiel might have responded with faith, by saying, "Why, yes, Lord, you say the word and it will be, just like at the creation." Or, on the other hand, he could have said cynically, "No way, God! This is the most lifeless place I've ever seen."

Instead, though perhaps doubtful, Ezekiel's answer is open-ended. He doesn't affirm that God has the power to make these bones live, but he doesn't deny it either. Not a bad answer: "God, it sounds like you've got something planned; let me step back to watch."

But Ezekiel realizes that he can't just stand back and watch. God *uses* Ezekiel to bring life back to the bones. "Prophesy," says the Lord. "Tell them that there is hope for new life. Tell them that they will have muscles again, and skin, and breath. Tell them that they are not dead. Tell them that there is hope."

So Ezekiel follows the Lord's command—even though he probably feels quite silly—and prophesies to the valley full of dry bones. And "suddenly there was a noise, a rattling, and the bones came together. . . . And there were sinews on them, and flesh had come upon them, and skin had covered them; but there was no breath in them" (vv. 7-8).

What, had Ezekiel not prophesied hard enough? Loudly enough? Forcefully enough?

How often do we hear the good news and don't take it all in? How often do we hear words of wholeness and let them pass us by? Or use a segment of what we hear, but not every part we need to absorb?

But it took only one more try. The Lord told Ezekiel exactly what to say to invite the four winds to come in and breathe life into the complete but lifeless bodies. And it was so. "The breath came into them, and they lived, and stood on their feet, a vast multitude" (v. 10).

But could the Lord not have spoken a word and the results have been the same, that all the bones would come together, and then muscles, and flesh, and skin, and breath? No, it appears that the Lord needed Ezekiel to tell the people that there was hope for the wilderness; that the people who were in a foreign land would one day be reconnected with their homeland; that there was hope for resurrection. Indeed, Ezekiel was an agent of resurrection. With the Lord's guidance, he brought hope and new life to people who felt desolate and dead.

We need each other. When we are in the desert, when we feel empty, when we feel parched as if nothing will satisfy our longings, we must depend on each other to bring the word from the Lord that will revive our souls. We, too, can be agents of resurrection.

In Psalm 130, from the depths the writer implores the Lord, "Let your ears be attentive to the voice of my supplications!" The story in Ezekiel tells us that the Lord hears our cries from the depths of our dryness and brokenness. The Lord hears, and the Lord provides agents of resurrection for us, people who remind us that life is not about death and dryness. Though we know, sometimes we need reminding that life is about accepting people as they are, not who we wish they would be. Life is about going out of our way to help someone, even when we think we don't have the time. Life is about spring, and the hope for renewal, because winter does pass. The flowers and trees did bloom last year. Baby birds were born, and life was renewed! Surely God will not desert us now. Even *our* sometimes lifeless bodies can have new life with God's breath inspiring us to reconnect, to become whole once again, so that shattering like a glass jar is no longer an option. God embraces us with steadfast love and redeeming power (Psalm 130:7), and encourages us, with faith, to be agents of resurrection and breathe new life into others.

# SUGGESTIONS FOR WORSHIP

## Call to Worship

| | |
|---|---|
| LEADER: | Out of the depths we cry to you, O Lord. |
| **PEOPLE:** | **Lord, hear our voices!** |
| LEADER: | Though you see the parts of us that feel dry, broken, or dead, revive us again this day. |
| **PEOPLE:** | **Call us forth to new life.** |
| **ALL:** | **Help us to respond as we center our hearts and our thoughts on you.** |

## Prayer of Confession

Holy Lord, we are nothing apart from you. We fail you in our actions and our thoughts, yet when we look toward you, even with our dim eyes, we see your steadfast and gracious love.

When we doubt, remind us of your faithfulness.

When we cry, embrace us with your comforting arms.

When we wish to die, breathe new life into us.

Forgive us, Lord, and renew us, we pray.

## Assurance of Pardon

God hears our cries from the depths of our hearts, and with grace, calls us back to rebirth and purity. Through the love of Jesus Christ, our sins are forgiven.

## Benediction

The steadfast love of God be with you as renewing Creator, resurrecting Christ, and energizing Spirit. Amen.

# Palm/Passion Sunday

Susan Steinberg

---

**Liturgy of the Palms:**

**Matthew 21:1-11:** Jesus' triumphal entry into Jerusalem.

**Psalm 118:1-2, 19-29:** The psalmist praises the one who comes in the name of the Lord.

**Liturgy of the Passion:**

**Isaiah 50:4-9***a***:** The servant's humiliation.

**Psalm 31:9-16:** The psalmist prays for God's mercy.

**Philippians 2:5-11:** The writer implores Christians to imitate the humility of Christ.

**Matthew 26:14–27:66:** The story of Jesus' passion and crucifixion.

---

## REFLECTIONS

No other Sunday in the Christian year is as laden with drama and emotion as Palm/Passion Sunday. We move from triumph to crucifixion, from faithfulness to betrayal, from devotion on the part of the women to agony on the lips of Jesus himself. This is a Sunday loaded with meaning—and full of possibilities for preaching.

With such a lengthy text to work with, the preacher must first choose one character or theme for the sermon. Remember: you cannot preach about all of it, and there will be other Palm/Passion Sundays. Also, the liturgy, the music, and the visual props of the day work with the sermon to create the appropriate moods and settings for the powerful narrative from the Gospel; the sermon does not need to carry the whole weight of the service. The sermon does not need to be long for this Sunday. In fact, considering the length of the text plus the other elements of the service, it should be shorter than usual. Word choice is crucial therefore.

While the service will often begin with a procession of palms and a reading of the entrance into Jerusalem from Matthew 21, by the time of the sermon the mood has changed. There is no question that the story is painful to hear, but most people are prepared for this to be a hard Sunday. The congregation is not looking for a light and easy Sunday at church. People expect to hear about Jesus' suffering and death, and they also expect the preacher to say a word about its meaning for them.

In this sermon, I chose to focus on atonement. I try to move from the text to a brief description of theory to the meaning of the cross for each of us today. During the service, a large wooden cross was carried in and placed at the foot of the steps leading up to the chancel; I was able to gesture toward the cross as I preached.

# A SERMON BRIEF

## "For You"

Each time we hear the story of the crucifixion of Jesus, questions arise. You cannot look at the cross without asking why; you can't face the cross without questioning its meaning. It is nearly impossible to stand in front of the cross and simply accept; the crucifixion begs reasoning. Why did Jesus die there? What is the purpose of the cross? When we hear the story, questions arise.

And so it is no wonder that pages and pages of Christian theology are devoted to the explanation of the cross. Over the centuries since Jesus cried out to God from Golgotha, Christian theologians have written books and volumes about the meaning of Christ's death.

One thing most of the writers agree on is that the crucifixion atones for our sins. Atonement, which breaks down as *at-one-ment*, is the reconciliation of two parties, the mending of the broken relationship between God and humanity. The cross, it is generally agreed, symbolizes atonement.

As with many theological issues, though, different atonement theories have evolved over time. According to the ransom theory of the early church, we are all slaves to sin; Christ died to ransom us from our captivity to evil. In the crucifixion, the theory goes, Jesus captures all of human evil and rescues us from original sin. But in the Middle Ages, theologians felt that the ransom theory gave too much power to the devil. So they developed the satisfaction theory. Theologians of the Middles Ages said that the problem is not so much that the great weight of human sin offends God. We are infinitely guilty, so much so that we consistently insult the infinite goodness of God. Jesus goes to the cross to satisfy God's wounded honor. The moral influence theory is a more modern concept of atonement. Authors of this theory feel that the other ideas don't give enough credit for human beings' capacity to change. This influence theory is popular among mainstream Protestants in North America—people like us like the idea that we can change. By pondering the passion of Christ we become aware of God's great love for us. The realization of such love influences us to change our lives for the better.[1]

Atonement: a ransom for our sin, satisfaction for our guilt, the influential sign of God's love. Over time, Christian thinkers have tried very hard to make sense of the cross.

But we are not here today to determine which atonement theory best fits our own belief system. We are not here to debate which theological suppositions we support and which we take issue with. For all the great theology of our tradition, the Gospel account of Christ's death was not written with theology in mind.

After all, we are not called to cling to theology; we are called to cling to Jesus Christ. Rather than wrap ourselves up in theory, as we look at the cross we must ask ourselves a very personal question: Do I believe Jesus died for me? Do I believe Jesus Christ was crucified for me? We do a pretty good job dodging that very personal approach. We struggle to believe Jesus suffered for us.

We can say with conviction, he did it for them. Why did Jesus suffer so? We talk easily about other people, and we should, because through Christ God can travel to the heart of suffering everywhere. We can point to the loss of life at the hands of cruel fate, here and around the world, knowing that in compassion Christ stands by all who mourn. Wherever violence claims the life of the innocent, wherever the justice system punishes people by death, wherever the suffering of the people makes no sense, Jesus is there.

Why did Jesus die on the cross? We can talk about God, and we should. Jesus was crucified for God. He was obedient unto death. Though he prayed to have the cup taken from him, he let God's will be done.

Christ's love of God and his love for all those who suffer and sin led him to the cross. All of this is true. But none of our talk has an impact on how we live our lives unless we believe that he laid down his life for us. Do you believe Jesus went to the cross for you? Can you trust that the crucifixion is about you?

We are almost at the end of Lent, our church season of self-examination. As you know, there are many ways of going about self-examination, many spiritual disciplines that open up the pages of your life and place them before God's gracious eyes. Some of you may have been practicing a form of discipline over the past six weeks. Ideally you have come to a greater self-understanding and a new awareness of God's love.

Yet perhaps some of you have discovered that one of the dangers of self-examination is that it can lead to self-punishment. In fact, one of the reasons many of us have trouble getting started with this kind of practice is that we don't believe God will still love us when we're through. Will God still love me if I bring to the surface my betrayals and doubts, my poor choices and regrets, my secrets and sorrows? Will God love me if I put my whole self under God's gaze? One of the risks of self-examination is that it can lead us to conclude for ourselves that we are beyond the reach of God's grace.

If you have imposed on yourself exclusion from the mercy of God, look at the cross. If you have presumed for yourself that you do not deserve the love of God, set your eyes on Christ. Rise above the cloud of your own self-determined unworthiness and gaze at the love of the cross. Start here when you start to wonder who you are in God's eyes. Look here and tremble. Jesus laid down his life for you—for you.

# SUGGESTIONS FOR WORSHIP

## Call to Worship (based on Psalm 118:26)

LEADER:     Blessed is the one who comes in the name of the Lord.
PEOPLE:     **Hosanna in the highest!**

## An Affirmation of Faith (based on Philippians 2:5-11)

Jesus Christ,
Though he was in the form of God,

*March 20, 2005*

Did not regard equality with God
As something to be exploited,
But emptied himself,
Taking the form of a slave,
Being born in human likeness.
And being found in human form
He humbled himself
And became obedient to the point of death—
Even death on a cross.

Therefore God also highly exalted him
And gave him the name that is above every name,
So that at the name of Jesus
Every knee should bend,
In heaven and on earth and under the earth,
And every tongue should confess to the glory of God:
Jesus Christ is Lord! Amen.

# Benediction

Go out into the world trusting that Jesus suffered and died for you.
Look to the cross and believe this: you are loved!

1. For a thorough discussion of these theories, see John Hall, *Professing the Faith* (Minneapolis: Fortress Press, 1993), 413-34.

# Holy Thursday

Susan Steinberg

---

**Exodus 12:1-4 (5-10), 11-14:** The first Passover celebration.

**Psalm 116:1-2, 12-19:** The psalmist praises the Lord "in the courts of the house of the Lord."

**1 Corinthians 11:23-26:** The institution of the Lord's Supper.

**John 13:1-17, 31b-35:** Jesus washes the disciples' feet as an example of his new commandment to "love one another."

---

## REFLECTIONS

Holy Thursday represents a welcome moment of grace during the painful procession of Holy Week services. Between Palm/Passion Sunday and Good Friday comes this graceful insertion of Jesus washing his disciples' feet. In spite of the political storm surrounding him, and the inevitability of his own painful death, he takes the time to give his friends one more sign of his love—and one more commandment to live by.

Protestants have never considered foot washing a sacrament, but in the Gospel of John this ritual takes the place of the Last Supper. Through this cleansing process, Jesus prepares himself and his disciples for his crucifixion. Jesus removes his outer robe and ties a towel around himself, signs that he is making himself ready for the cross. By cleaning his disciples' feet, he demonstrates not only his love for them but also how they are to love one another when he is gone.

The Holy Thursday service is solemn, yet not as stark as Good Friday. The preacher may even feel like including a bit of humor—if carefully considered. Grace is abundant and needs to be communicated at this point in Holy Week. Foot washing is still not common, though it probably would do Protestant congregations well to get into the habit. Communion is usually served, however. Grace comes through the Lord's Supper, of course, but it should come through in the sermon as well.

In this sermon, I focus on foot washing as a sacramental vision, a vision of Christian community. Jesus commands us to love one another as he has loved us: he commands us to welcome one another with grace and a place to sit in spite of the stink of our sandals and the grit between our toes.

# A SERMON BRIEF

## "Between the Toes"

My preschool-age daughter and I have a nighttime routine: we rub each other's feet with peppermint foot lotion. I don't know how it got started, but I do know I don't want it to end. I cherish those moments when she lathers my sore feet with tingly pink stuff; and she loves the feeling on her young, soft skin. "Between my toes!" she demands, when she wants the full treatment.

Few things can match the sensation of a good foot rub, or even better, foot cleaning. Clean feet feel extra good after a long day in a hot and dusty location. Whether it's a day on the Appalachian trail or a day in a city like Managua, nothing beats dunking dirt-caked feet in a tub of cold water to make you feel like a new person.

If you ever traveled to Central America or the Holy Land or any place where your feet absorb grime morning to night, you know what the disciples' feet looked like at the end of the day. Out walking around all day in sandals left their feet covered with crusty evidence of countless dirt roads. Even when they peeled their sandals off in the evening they could see exactly where the straps had been. Nothing would have felt better to the disciples than a thorough foot washing. A soak and a rub, and they would have been ready for anything.

Here at the end of his life, Jesus knows exactly how to show his disciples how much he loves them. "Having loved his own who were in the world," the Gospel says, "he loved them to the end." How does he demonstrate his love? He washes their feet.

The scene of Jesus pouring water over his disciples' filthy feet is one of the most intimate portraits of Jesus we have. As often as he seems disgruntled by the disciples' dopiness, now he appears as gentle and gracious as their best friend. Through this simple but intensely personal cleansing event, Jesus draws closer than ever to his disciples in his final hours.

Yet there is much more to Jesus' intent than leaving his friends with a good feeling. Jesus has a lot more in mind. He uses the powerful gesture of foot washing as a pre-crucifixion rite. The Gospel of John has no Last Supper, no words of institution: foot washing is it. Where the other Gospels report a last meal, John tells of a final foot washing. By calling his disciples together and kneeling before them to wash them off, Jesus is getting them all ready for his crucifixion.

Peter—and perhaps he speaks for the others—balks at the idea of his master washing his lowly feet, but Jesus tells him, "Unless I wash you, you have no share with me." "If you don't go through this with me," Jesus seems to say, "you're not part of my kingdom"; "If you don't let me turn authority on its head, you can't participate in my new way of ordering the world." Then of course Peter wants his whole body to be washed—he doesn't want to miss out.

Jesus' time to depart is coming fast, and he has to make a final impression. He chooses the ritual of foot washing. It is a wonderful sensation, yes, but Jesus has more in mind. He doesn't just offer to wipe the dirt off his disciples' feet—he makes it an ultimatum. "Let me wash you clean, or else knowing me leads to nothing; let me be the one to clean up your life, or else your connection with me is fruitless."

Accepting foot washing means going all the way to Golgotha with Jesus. Letting him take hold of your stinky toes translates into giving your whole self over to him, wherever it may lead. His washing of your feet is not just a casual encounter among friends—it is making a choice about how you go forward into whatever lies ahead. As a poet said about the choices we make: "To know our ambiguity and yet to live into the light."[1] Allowing Jesus to get close enough to wash your dirtiest dirt away is a choice you must make in the shadow of the night.

But foot washing is also more than a personal call to follow Christ; it is more than a one-on-one process. Jesus lays before the disciples a sacramental vision: a vision of the promises between God and us, a vision of Christian community at its best. While foot washing has never qualified as a sacrament in the Protestant tradition, we certainly can call it sacramental.

We need such visions, visions of what we are striving for, visions of how God wants us to live with one another. In Wendell Berry's profound novel *Jayber Crow*, the main character is the town barber who is also the church janitor—or sexton, as we prefer to say. After several years serving the church, he has an epiphany about the congregation he knows so well. An overwhelming vision takes hold of him, and he sees the gathered community "perfected beyond time by one another's love."[2] It is a vision of the community as it will never be: perfect. But what Jayber Crow sees is powerful enough to feed his faith and keep him moving toward something better than the present.

Jesus leaves the disciples, and all of us, that sort of vision. His parting gift to us all is a stunning image of Christian community at its best: brothers and sisters in Christ loving one another as he has loved us. Jesus bestows on us a picture of his commandment to love one another: a picture of believers graciously washing one another's feet clean no matter what our heritage, title, or training; a picture of the faithful unafraid of wiping away the grit between one another's toes. We will never experience the Christian community perfected beyond time, but we can choose to live with the sacramental vision of Holy Thursday as our guide. Amen.

# SUGGESTIONS FOR WORSHIP

## Call to Worship (based on Psalm 116)

LEADER:     I love the Lord, because he has heard my voice and my supplication.

**PEOPLE:**     **He inclined his ear to me, therefore I will call on him as long as I live.**

LEADER:     I will lift up the cup of salvation and call on the name of the Lord.

**PEOPLE:**     **I will pay my vows to the Lord in the presence of all his people.**

ALL:     **Praise the Lord!**

## Prayer of Confession

God of grace, we confess that we have not loved one another as you have loved us. We have neglected the needs of those around us, and ignored the plight of the poor. Forgive us, we pray, for denying your claim on our lives. Draw us closer to you, even now as we seek new life through your son, Jesus Christ.

## Benediction

Brothers and sisters, love one another as Jesus loves you. By this everyone will know you are Christ's disciples, if you love one another. Go in peace to love and serve God.

1. Jennifer Lynn Woodruff, "Winter Sunset," in *Weavings* vol. 17, no. 1 (January/February 2002), 22.
2. Wendell Berry, *Jayber Crow* (New York: Counterpoint Press, 2000), 205.

# Resurrection of the Lord/ Easter Day

Jill Y. Crainshaw

---

**Acts 10:34-43:** Peter proclaims the good news of Jesus Christ to the Gentiles.

**Psalm 118:1-2, 14-24:** The "gates of righteousness" have been opened to God's people.

**Colossians 3:1-4:** Being "raised with Christ" means our minds are turned to "things that are above."

**John 20:1-18:** Mary Magdalene discovers the empty tomb and then encounters the risen Lord.

---

## REFLECTIONS

The liturgical year symbolically insists that Easter overflows the edges of one Sunday to last fifty days. The Sundays following Resurrection Sunday are not Sundays *after* Easter. They are the Sundays *of* Easter. What this means is that Easter Day is not the end of the Lenten penitential season. It is the beginning of a period of seven weeks full of liturgical opportunities to vocalize the gospel melody of resurrection hope.

A vital dimension of the Easter lectionary is the opportunity it provides to draw worshipers more deeply into the meaning of "joy." On Easter Sunday, resurrection sunrise again and again each year caresses the earth with its light and invites response: What does the church's language of "alive again" mean? What is "joy" in this world where so many people suffer daily crucifixions? What lyric will the contemporary church put to the hymn of resurrection so that it offers meaning and hope to a hurting world?

97

A danger of Easter Sunday worship and preaching is to romanticize Easter through theologically thin celebrations, celebrations that only skim the surface of the resurrection's cosmic breadth and depth. Mary's story in John 20 beckons us to a deeper experience of Easter faith by reminding us of the importance of developing a substantive theology of joy that does not triumphalistically minimize the reality of human suffering and pain.

The resurrection narratives, beginning with John 20:1-18 on this Sunday and continuing throughout the fifty days of Easter, stretch minds and imaginations to consider that the limits of the human mind cannot contain what God sets free. Beginning the fifty days of Easter this year by exploring with Mary the meaning of joy can give faith a deeper vision in which the unexpected rhythms of redemption break through in the voices and events of daily resurrections.

# A SERMON BRIEF

## "The Irony of Gardens and Graveyards: Some Bittersweet Reflections on Resurrection"

The truth will set you free, but first it will shatter the safe, sweet way you live.

—Sue Monk Kidd[1]

Early on the first day of the week, while it was still dark, Mary Magdalene went to the graveyard, and what did she find growing there? What she found growing there was bittersweet. The bittersweet irony of the resurrection. The bittersweet irony of gardens in graveyards. The bittersweet irony of what the church is called to preach, if we dare: "The truth will set you free, but first it will shatter the safe, sweet way you live."

One night as the choir ran up and down its scales in our little country church, we kids ran up and down the dirt road out back. It was summer, time for that favorite childhood game, hide-and-seek, and that dumb ole Randy had challenged me. Even at age ten, I balked when anyone tried to tell me what girls can and cannot do. I declared defiantly, "I'll hide so good you'll never find me."

It was the best hiding place ever. Way in the corner of the ball field was a picnic shelter. I shinnied up the pole into the rafters and waited. After a while, I heard them, voices echoing closer. Finally, Randy and the others sat on the picnic table, my feet dangling just over their heads. "Well, she's not here," I heard Randy say, and they ran off giggling to hunt some more. I grinned and sat there in the best hiding place ever. Minutes crept by and I sat there, smug and swatting mosquitoes, in the best hiding place ever. Many more minutes later, I still sat there, bored and swatting mosquitoes, in the best hiding place ever. Finally, hot and itching I ran back to the church and there in the nursery sat my friends playing tic-tac-toe.

"What are ya'll doing in here?"

Randy answered, "We couldn't find you, and we got tired of looking. I guess you win."

I stood silent for a moment. It was the best hiding place ever—and the emptiest victory. I think Robert Fulghum's exegesis of a similar childhood experience contains much wisdom: in the end, whether they realize it or not, most people really want to be found.

The words dance off the pages of countless Easter sermons. In the resurrection we encounter God's gift of grace. Grace. It means being found by a love that never stops looking for us. Grace. It is one of the most reassuring promises of faith, and in our world. Some people long to hear the sweet sound of grace wrapping its melody around the chaos. Some people long to be found.

Not too long ago, however, I was reading John 20:1-18 in October in preparation for an ordination sermon, and I was struck by unexpected discord. Reading this resurrection narrative by the light of autumn's fiery glow instead of to the trumpeting doxologies of springtime's daffodils changed the tone and timbre of the story in ways that were both unexpected and profound. Reading the familiar words, I caught a glimpse of what is startlingly unfamiliar about this text. Mary Magdalene is found; but when a person is found in the way that Mary is found in John 20, that kind of being found can plunge us beneath the triumphant surface waters of the resurrection into mystifying depths we never even knew were there. And it is in those murky depths that we are challenged by prophetic realities: God calls people we never even considered before to do God's work. Baptismal naming happens in unlikely places such as graveyards and chases away forever the labels the world imposes. The resurrection does not make crucifixions okay. Murky depths, but it is in these prophetic depths that we find the courage to announce God's news of resurrection hope.

Is it possible that John's resurrection narrative is luring us into those deeper waters to consider a different kind of alleluia, to risk catching sight of something we don't usually see when the words are all dressed up in Easter Sunday's bright colors? Could it be that John's narrative is nudging us toward the haunting depths of a more profound truth?

Early on the first day of the week, in the graveyard, Mary sees a gardener. Questions tumble treacherously off the page and into our pathway. Consider: What kind of foliage is this gardener nurturing in a graveyard garden? What does this gardener's language of resurrection mean to Mary Magdalene who came to the graveyard determined to face her pain, no matter how dark and terrible it seemed? What does faith's language of "alive again" mean to those whose pain is so deep they reel awkwardly from the edge of one abyss to another, disoriented, frightened, and confused? In a wilderness world like ours, how does that creek on God's eternal mountain break free to run with giggling abandon through farmlands and cities, reconciling divided hearts and bringing peace?

The unexpected appearance of these kinds of questions stirs the realization. Being called to preach? That was not what Mary longed for when she stumbled wearily through the morning darkness. She loved Jesus with a fierce love. To get that love back was her soul's deep longing. So, being called to preach? Preaching was the furthest thing from Mary's mind. Even so, the question the gardener asks her is the same question Jesus asks the first disciples when he calls them to follow him in John 1: "Who are you looking for?" Mary's response in 20:18 is the same response Paul makes to validate his apostleship after the Damascus road experience: "I have seen the Lord." Peter. Paul. And Mary? Called to preach? Perhaps, but that was not Mary's heart cry that morning.

Mary went to the garden in the graveyard longing to be found. She is found, but the truth of what that means is bittersweet. The gardener cannot give her what she longs for. The way that she loved Jesus must be replanted in different soil, nurtured in a different way. And that, it seems, is the irony of the ministry to which we are called. Think about it. What is really going on in this story? Resurrection? Perhaps. Mary courageously struggling to face head-on the reality of suffering and death? Perhaps. Is it even possible that in a hauntingly unexpected way the gardener longs to be found too, to be set free to live his truth in the same way that Jesus set lepers and prostitutes free to claim the power of their own names? Perhaps.

Then the baptismal irony tumbles from the gardener's mouth: "Mary." The gardener speaks her name, and I can only imagine that the deep soil of that graveyard garden rejoiced as truth set them both free—the radical, prophetic truth of God's resurrection grace.

In the backyard of a house I lived in several years ago was a patch of dirt that resisted all growth. A determined gardener, I planted all sorts of grass and flowers. Nothing took root and nothing grew—except a vine-like plant with red berries that was already there. It wrapped its arms around a tree nearby and grew like crazy. It was colorful and pretty, in a way, but I carried in my heart the resolve of a weekend gardener to transform that patch of dirt into a luscious jungle of flowering vegetation. It was that stubborn resolve that sprouted my decision to cut back the vine on the off-chance that it was choking out other plants. A friend stopped by in the midst of my labors and asked me what I was doing. I learned an unexpected truth from my friend that day. The red-berried vine that grew with such grace and vitality in the poor soil has a name—"bittersweet." Allowed to grow, it is splendid in its proclamation of the irony: gardens can grow in graveyards.

Early on the first day of the week, while it was still dark, Mary Magdalene went to the graveyard, and what did she find growing there? Bittersweet. The bittersweet irony of what we are called to preach—if we dare. And that is the bittersweet irony of gardens and graveyards; the truth will set you free, but first it will shatter the safe sweet way you live. We are called. Let us go and announce the news.

# SUGGESTIONS FOR WORSHIP

## Call to Worship

Several years ago, while in a waiting room, I read a poem that contained some of the language of this call to worship. Even though I have never seen the poem again, pieces of it have stayed with me, surfacing in this Easter litany. I credit the poet, whose name I do not remember but whose artistic rendering stoked the embers of my faith.

VOICE 1: "This is the day that the Lord has made; let us rejoice and be glad in it" (Psalm 118:24).

VOICE 2: Tiptoeing across the fields on a spring-warm day, the rain comes—splashing, dripping, drenching the earth.

VOICE 1: And in the forest? Daffodils trumpet out the good news.

VOICE 2: Christ is the resurrection and the life!

ALL:             **Christ is the resurrection and the life!**

*(Here it may be appropriate to sing one verse of an Easter hymn. An example is "Christ the Lord Is Risen Today." After the first verse, the litany continues.)*

VOICE 1:         Gently, like the morning dew, God's love caresses longing spirits—splashing, dripping, drenching eager hearts.

VOICE 2:         And in God's church? The promise of new life stirs the good news.
                 Buried dreams, forgotten hopes, embers ready to flame into new life.
                 Icy hearts, frozen souls, melted by the Light of the World.

VOICE 1:         Christ is the resurrection and the life!

ALL:             **Christ is the resurrection and the life!**

*(Insert the next verse of the hymn.)*

VOICE 2:         Joyfully, like a springtime creek, God's grace flows out—splashing, dripping, cascading into the world.

VOICE 1:         And in God's church, in God's people, hope is born.

VOICE 2:         Christ is the resurrection and the life!

ALL:             **Christ is the resurrection and the life!**

*(Insert the final verse of the hymn.)*

VOICE 1:         "This is the day that the Lord has made; let us rejoice and be glad in it."

# Benediction (based on John 20)

We have seen the Lord! Go and announce the news. Christ is the resurrection and the life. Alleluia! Alleluia!

1. Sue Monk Kidd, *The Dance of the Dissident Daughter* (New York: HarperCollins, 1996).

# Second Sunday of Easter

### Claire Smith

---

**Acts 2:14a, 22-32:** Peter addresses the crowd on the day of Pentecost, preaching the good news of Christ's resurrection.

**Psalm 16:** The psalmist sings a song of trust and security that is found in God.

**1 Peter 1:3-9:** Despite their trials, those who trust in the power of God as revealed in Jesus Christ have been granted "a new birth into a living hope."

**John 20:19-31:** The disciples are confronted by the risen Christ, and generations of believers are blessed by Christ for believing without seeing.

---

## REFLECTIONS

Silence fell;
Deep, deafening silence.
It could not be.

Phantom,
Spirit,
They thought.

Deep within
They wondered.
What did the apparition mean?

It was the last straw!

Jesus, gone.
Fear seized them in its grip!
The authorities . . .

Afraid of prison, afraid of death
And now this!
It could not be.

Maybe?
No! The door was still secured.

Then it spoke!
Peace
Peace be with you.

At last
That old, accustomed voice.

His hands, his side
Plain to see.

And suddenly,
They knew

Knew it was
The RESURRECTED LORD
In all his power and might.

Joy replaced fear
Peace
Hope

But he was not done.
Go, he said,
I send you, as God sent me.

Awesome task.
Still he was not done
Receive the Holy Spirit.

Spirit of power
Spirit of truth
Spirit of righteousness
Spirit of counsel.

Still he was not done.
Power to forgive or
Not forgive.

As he was sent—
He forgave.

Still he was not done.
Thomas.

Through him
Jesus speaks to all

Resurrection
Peace
Power

It is not done.

# A SERMON BRIEF

## "Can It End?"

Where did it end? Some would have said the minute Jesus "bucked" the Pharisees, it was only a matter of time. Some would have said the minute he "ran wild" in the temple, it was only a matter of time—the beginning of the end, in fact. Some would have said when he was arrested, again, the beginning of the end. Some would have said at the crucifixion. It was definitely the end. But was it? There was still the resurrection. And for some, that would have been the end. For others, the ascension. However, the Gospel text from John makes it evident that there is no end.

The disciples were fearful of the authorities. They sought comfort in each other. They could reminisce and wonder and dream together. They had shared so much with the master. They went into a room by themselves. Into that room Jesus came and showed that the end had not come. Jesus showed them this by giving them four things.

First, Jesus gave them peace. He came in the midst of their insecurity, disappointment, disillusionment, frustration, and fear. The locked doors represented all these. Jesus walked right through those doors in all his resurrected power, entered into their turmoil as he had done before, and spoke peace to them. These were words Jesus had spoken to them previously. Consequently, they contained a double assurance. It was not only that Jesus was powerful; it was not only that they had witnessed an event with which nothing could compare; it was not only that the presence of Jesus could calm their fear—it was more than that. Jesus had kept his promise to come back to them, albeit for a short while. For when Jesus had spoken these words before, it had been in the context of his leaving and returning and sending the Holy Spirit. Moreover, it was in the context of Jesus seeking to allay their future fears. If they did not want to believe Mary or anybody else, they could not doubt the presence of Jesus himself. Now he came and once again spoke "Peace." That was not the only thing Jesus said and gave.

Jesus came and gave them a mission: "As the Father has sent me, so send I you." A simple, short sentence, loaded with meaning. God sent Jesus in obedience, in humility, in service. Obedience to God, humility before all, and service to all. Moreover, God sent Jesus in truth. Jesus was true to his mission, and spoke and lived words of righteousness as God defines righteousness. This was not an easy mission to fulfill. The climate was hostile. They knew they were not Jesus, full of mighty words and deeds. Indeed, some of them had failed him at the most critical moments. They were locked away in fear. Thus Jesus gave them the promised Holy Spirit.

Earlier, in John 14:26, Jesus had promised the Spirit in the same context in which he had given them peace—a peace that was different from what the world gave. Jesus' earlier discourses concerning the Holy Spirit show that in giving the Spirit, Jesus dealt with the disciples' need for presence, guidance, teaching, authority, and power. Although Jesus had returned, he could not stay with them. He had to leave until his appointed time when he came to establish his kingdom. Jesus understood where his disciples were, knew what they needed. He didn't give them an important mission because he had any illusions about them. But they had followed him, shared in his life and ministry with all its challenges and danger, and remained together after he left, inspired by their memories of him. These were the people he had trained by precept and example. He knew their capabilities by themselves. More than that, he knew their capabilities under the power of the Holy Spirit. "Receive the Holy Spirit," he said.

And with the Holy Spirit Jesus gave them authority. It is such a fascinating statement—"If you forgive the sins of any, they are forgiven them; if you retain the sins of any, they are retained" (John 20:23).

106

They convey authority, not license. The disciples were sent as Jesus was sent. Jesus taught grace and forgiveness, demonstrated it and encouraged it among his disciples. This is his intent. On the cross, he said of his bitterest enemies, "Father, forgive them; for they do not know what they are doing" (Luke 23:34). The authority represented his trust in his disciples.

As we speak of disciples, we remember that one, Thomas, was missing. However, he did not miss out. The resurrected Christ put in a special appearance for Thomas and then used him to speak to others—even us. Through Thomas, Jesus ensured that all his ensuing disciples would understand that they also have been given peace, and the Holy Spirit, and authority. Through Thomas, disciples for generations to come would understand that they also have been sent out with a mission, as the Father sent Christ, and as Christ now sends them.

It cannot end. It continues with us. We are part of the continuing story. Who among us has not faced insecurity, disappointment, disillusionment, frustration, and fear? Sometimes our struggles are the result of our own personal inhibitions. Sometimes they are caused by the people around us. And sometimes life just seems to treat us unfairly. There are times when we feel inadequate; there are times when no one seems to care. There are times when it appears that those around us couldn't care whether or not there is a God, much less seek to honor God. There are even times when we wonder if Jesus is real. No matter our state of mind, Jesus still says "Peace." Jesus still speaks to the things that disturb us, and sends us as the Father sent him: to be obedient to God, humble before all, and to serve all. Jesus has breathed upon us, and we have received the Holy Spirit. We have received authority to minister in Jesus' name. Let us go with this commitment—it shall not end.

# Call to Worship

LEADER:      Blessed be the Lord, God Almighty!
                  Blessed be our Lord and Saviour Jesus Christ!
                  Blessed be the Holy Spirit of truth!
PEOPLE:     **Christ has risen from the dead**
                  **And sits at the right hand of God.**
                  **We are glad and rejoice in the life God has given us.**
ALL:          **Alleluia!**

# Litany

| | |
|---|---|
| LEADER: | God, you are our refuge; |
| **PEOPLE:** | **You are our God, our portion.** |
| LEADER: | We bless you for your guidance, |
| **PEOPLE:** | **You are always with us.** |
| LEADER: | We praise you for your presence; |
| **PEOPLE:** | **You are our life and our joy.** |
| LEADER: | We thank you for your steadfastness and love; |
| **PEOPLE:** | **We thank you for Jesus Christ,** |
| LEADER: | That he died and rose again. |
| **PEOPLE:** | **You have given us salvation.** |
| LEADER: | Teach us to live in ways that please you. |
| **PEOPLE:** | **May our lives be a fragrant offering to you;** |
| LEADER: | May you be glorified in us. |
| **ALL:** | **Amen.** |

# Benediction

May the God who sends, the Spirit who empowers, and the Christ who redeems strengthen you to do God's will. Go in the name of God our Parent, Jesus our Brother, and the Holy Spirit. Go.

# Third Sunday of Easter

### Maggie Lauterer

---

**Acts 2:14a, 36-41:** Peter preaches a message of repentance and baptism, and three thousand new believers join the early Christians.

**Psalm 116:1-4, 12-19:** The Lord has heard the psalmist's prayer, and the psalmist asks, "What shall I return to the LORD for all [the Lord's] bounty to me?"

**1 Peter 1:17-23:** Peter calls Christian believers to a life of holy living and faith.

**Luke 24:13-35:** The risen Christ appears to two travelers on the road to Emmaus.

---

## REFLECTIONS

This is one of my favorite stories in the New Testament. There is a remarkable intimacy here. Two guys, like extras in a film, are faces in the crowd, but suddenly and unexpectedly receive close and animated attention by the star, the one who plays the leading role. It is a fantasy we all could have, the fantasy of encountering our Lord Jesus in the flesh. But the inability of the two to recognize Jesus is the part of the story that haunts us. What if we fell into the same trap? And why would we?

It is a story of traveling down an unpaved, long and dusty road, filled with doubt and questions. The journey of Cleopas and his unnamed friend (who could be you or me), speaks strongly to us, those who also have vicariously watched the events of Holy Week unfold. We identify with their journey, but for a whole different set of reasons.

# A SERMON BRIEF

## "Where Do We Go from Here?"

I'm from the generation that loved to sit around with a guitar strumming and sing folk songs, both old and new. To this day one of our favorite "new" songs is by Tom Paxton. The song is *I Can't Help But Wonder Where I'm Bound*. It's about traveling down a dusty road, not knowing where you're going. It's about the agony of the road and wondering if you will ever feel that you have arrived home.

I can almost imagine those two travelers walking down the road that Easter afternoon, singing that song and wondering—wondering where they were bound. In one sense, I don't think they knew where they were bound. Sure, they knew they were on their way to Emmaus—a little town about seven miles outside of Jerusalem. But look closely and you will find the hidden and unasked question: "Where do we go from here?"

On this third Sunday of Easter, we are on that long, dusty road with the two travelers. I don't think we have any choice. We Christians can't just give each other lilies and dyed eggs on Easter Sunday and be done with it. We are compelled to stand with our arms lifted to the heavens, dazed with the news. We travel along in Eastertide for weeks, reveling in and reeling with the radical new reality brought about by the resurrection. And we sing about Easter and the resurrection all the way to Ascension Day, only a couple of weeks from now. So we cling to the hem of the risen Christ's garment, amazed, relieved, with what seems to be the same question, "Where do we go from here?" But our question and the travelers' question are not quite the same. Let me explain.

Those two travelers were asking that question for a very specific reason: they were lost. These were two men who were not main characters in the Holy Week drama. They were simply two people who stood on the fringe of the crowd, drawn to this man, Jesus, and his teachings, but not willing to call him more than a prophet. With the trial and death of Christ, those "hopes" were dashed; and so they're leaving Jerusalem, literally walking away from the scene, stumbling over their dashed hopes, and oblivious to the reality of the risen Christ.

It was on that solemn trip, wrapped up as they were in their own thoughts and conversation, that the sacred Stranger caught up with them. You can almost hear the sound of his sandals on the road.

110

On that dusty way, they opened their disappointments to this stranger. They wondered where they were bound. "We had hoped he was the one. . . ." They had hoped they were going in the right direction, on the road to believing he might be the Messiah. But it was only a hope.

If the "hope" they had in this Jesus had been so intense, why were they not able to recognize him? They seemed to know every detail, every event of the past week. But, still, they could not recognize the central figure as he walked by their side. Had the shroud of discouragement darkened the way? Were they so close to their own little world of disappointment that they could not see clearly?

How blessed those travelers were that the risen Christ himself lengthened his stride, caught up, and walked with them as he explained the whole story from Moses and the Prophets to the sacrifice of the lamb without blemish to the outpouring of God's mercy and grace in the resurrection. They had to walk the complete seven dusty miles to the little town of Emmaus and to invite the stranger to sit and eat with them before their eyes would be opened to recognize the Christ as their companion on the road.

I meet people who express the same kind of disappointment that Cleopas and his friend expressed to Jesus. "I had hoped that Jesus was the Messiah in my life . . ." they'll say and shake their heads. But often they are like the travelers, too busy in their own questions and puzzlement to realize that they already enjoy the companionship of the master.

Perhaps that is where we are meant to go from here. Perhaps we are meant to break through the skepticism of a world blinded by despair and disappointment. If we really do believe that Jesus Christ burst the chains of death, what do we do with this remarkable good news? How would Jesus have us live it out on the road of life? Where would God have us to carry it? We can only answer that question within the deepest places of our own hearts and faith. But one thing is certain: we can't help but continue to wander, to wander out into the world to share the good news of the one who walks with us on our journeys of faith. Why? Because we have no choice; we too have encountered the risen Christ and all he means for our lives and world. And like the travelers on the road to Emmaus, our hearts are burning within us, burning to share that good news. So where can we go this Easter season but out into the world that so desperately needs to hear the message of those first Easter witnesses: "The Lord has risen indeed!" (v. 34).

# SUGGESTIONS FOR WORSHIP

## Call to Worship

LEADER: Let us come walk with the Lord.

**PEOPLE:** **Let us shake the dust of other travels from our shoes and go the new road with the risen Christ.**

LEADER: May our eyes be opened to recognize his presence by our side.

**PEOPLE:** **In this Eastertide, let us celebrate that Christ is risen and walks with us!**

**ALL:** **Christ is risen indeed!**

## Prayer of Confession

Good and gracious God, hear our prayer. We confess that as we journey along the road of our lives, we often lose our way. It is because we do not recognize the signs of your presence. We are caught up in our own small-mindedness, our own frustrations, our own stubbornness, refusing to lift up our eyes to the Light. Forgive our self-imposed blindness, that we may see clearly the road you have set out for us. In the name of Jesus, who walks the road with us. Amen.

## Assurance of Pardon

LEADER: The grace of God overflowed for us with the faith and love that are in Christ Jesus.

**PEOPLE:** **Christ came into the world to save sinners. For that very reason we received mercy, making us an example to those who would come to believe in him for eternal life. To the king of the ages, immortal, invisible, the only God, be honor and glory forever and ever. Amen.**

**ALL:** **Thanks be to God!**

## Benediction

May the risen Christ walk with you as you journey forth in his name to share the good news of his grace. Amen.

# Fourth Sunday of Easter

Stacey Simpson Duke

---

**Acts 2:42-47:** Christian believers shared a common life of worship and good deeds.

**Psalm 23:** The shepherd psalm.

**1 Peter 2:19-25:** Peter encourages believers to endure suffering according to the example of Christ.

**John 10:1-10:** Jesus describes himself as the shepherd who guards his sheep.

---

## REFLECTIONS

It would be difficult to find a more beloved and more familiar scripture passage than Psalm 23. Even people who have never darkened the door of a church or synagogue can quote this psalm from memory. They've heard it at funerals, in hospital rooms, even on television soap operas. People love this text with good reason. Many of them know it as well as the preacher does. Preaching it can present a unique challenge because it can seem as if there is nothing new to say.

As I write this, a sniper has assassinated nine people in the Washington, D.C., area one by one and remains at-large. A nightclub in Bali was bombed this past weekend, and nearly two hundred people died instantly. Our nation observed the first anniversary of September 11 just last month. Our government is sending every signal that our nation is on the brink of war with Iraq. Our economy continues in a downward spiral. We have countless reasons to be afraid and countless reasons to grieve.

In such a context, Psalm 23 speaks as clearly and relevantly as ever. The psalmist takes seriously the evil of this world and nevertheless holds fast to trust in God. In such a time as this, *new* news isn't necessarily what people need; *good* news is. The ancient, trustworthy words of this psalm are exactly what people need and want to hear. I see my task as preacher to be that of helping people reconnect with the powerful truths of this psalm.

The psalm doesn't ask to be interpreted or explained. It asks to be heard. It asks to be trusted. It asks to be claimed.

# A SERMON BRIEF

It was my grandmother who taught me how not to be afraid.

As a child, I was afraid of everything—the dark, the thunder, the ocean, the bogeyman. Nothing my parents said to me could put my little mind at ease. That's the way fear is. It does not listen to reason. It can take on a life of its own. My fear was huge.

When I was eight years old, my grandmother moved in with us. The first year she lived with us she slept on a daybed in the living room. That Christmas Eve, though, she came and slept with me, because the Christmas tree was in the living room, and she wanted to stay out of Santa's way. She and I lay there in my bed that night in the dark, looking up at the ceiling and whispering to each other while the rest of the house slept. I felt so safe with her there, until she started to fall asleep. Then all my fears started kicking in, until I couldn't stand it anymore and finally cried out, "Granna, I'm scared!"

Granna didn't try to tell me all the good and rational reasons not to be afraid: our neighborhood was safe, our doors were locked, our dog would protect us. She didn't try to talk me out of my fear. She didn't even tell me that Christmastime was no time for a little girl to be scared. Instead she taught me a Bible verse: "What time I am afraid, I will trust in thee. Psalm 56:3" (KJV). She had me say it just like that, over and over, until I knew it by heart. I lay there staring into the dark, saying those words aloud, partly rhyme, partly prayer, until I knew not just the words, but a little bit of what they meant too. Somehow saying I trusted made it already sort of true.

The same thing happens when we speak the words of Psalm 23. When do we recite this psalm? When we're scared, when we're sad, when we're down to our last hope. Yet what we say is this: "I shall not want"; "I fear no evil"; "My cup runs over." In the midst of our worst times, we make these affirmations that run counter to what our situation tells us is reality. This psalm has such power partly because the psalmist puts these truths in the declarative. The psalmist doesn't pat us on the hand and sweetly tell us, "Do not fear. God is with you." The psalmist doesn't tell us all the reasons it is silly to be scared or sad. Instead, the psalmist acknowledges that we humans can end up stumbling through some very dark valleys. He states that reality and then declares, and invites us to declare, "I shall not fear! You are with me!" Somehow saying it makes it already partly true.

I no longer fear the dark, the thunder, the ocean, the bogeyman. For the most part, my fears are more "adult" now. Terrorism. War. Random violence. Financial setback. Cancer. There are plenty of reasons to be afraid, and more than enough reasons to grieve. Terrible things happen in our world, and we are vulnerable to them. Even if nothing tragic were ever to happen in our lives, to be human means at least this: we are all going to die, and so is everyone we love.

The psalmist knows all this. He doesn't try to convince us otherwise. He doesn't pretend. He acknowledges that awful shadow. He acknowledges the reality of enemies. He acknowledges that sometimes life gets almost as dark as death. But what he knows is that there's something more.

With the dark shadow hanging over us all, the psalmist puts words in our mouths that change everything: *I shall not want. I fear no evil, for God is with me. God is my comfort. God provides for me in the midst of all trouble. My cup runs over.* The psalmist grabs us by the chin, turns our head, and points our eyes toward all the goodness and all the mercy that follow us. "Yes, see the shadow," the psalmist says, "it's dark, it's awful, it's scary, it's real. But look! Look at what else is here. Look at all this goodness. Look at all this mercy. Look at how the Holy One is right here with you! Look at all this beautiful, beautiful life."

In the midst of life we are in death, the *Book of Common Prayer* tells us. Yes, but in the midst of death we are in life, the psalmist reminds us.

There is so much death all around us. But there is so much life! Look around. Babies are born, and people fall in love, sea turtles lay their eggs, and symphonies are composed, addicts quit using, and salmon keep swimming upstream. Terrible things happen, but so many beautiful things are happening too—all of them a sign of God's continuing goodness and mercy.

Be grateful. Take none of this for granted. God's goodness is everywhere. God's mercy is all around. Our cups overflow. The world is so beautiful. Life is so beautiful. Fear is a choice. So is gratitude. So is trust.

When life gets very dark, when the world gets very scary, it helps to speak the words of our faith, even if we have to do it through gritted teeth. We don't say those words alone. We say them with the psalmist, we say them with our grandmothers, we say them with all the saints.

Why not say the words again? Say them now, or say them in the dark before you sleep. Say them aloud, or say them in the quiet of your own heart. *Though I walk through the darkest valley, I fear no evil; for you are with me. I fear no evil, for you are with me.* Maybe you will find what I have found, that saying it makes it feel already true. Because it is.

# SUGGESTIONS FOR WORSHIP

## Call to Worship (based on Psalm 23:5-6)

LEADER:      Come let us worship the Lord our God. God has pre-pared a table before us in the presence of all opposi-tion.

PEOPLE:      **God has anointed our heads with oil; our cups overflow.**

LEADER:      Surely goodness and mercy will follow us all the days of our lives.

PEOPLE:      **And we shall dwell in the house of the Lord for-ever.**

LEADER:      Come let us worship the Lord our God.

## Prayer of Confession

Generous God, you have called us to awe and gratitude, but too often we exist only on the surface, living lives that do not reflect your deep grace. Forgive us our lack of wonder. Forgive us for tripping through life without attending to your little miracles all around us. Forgive us for grasping our lives as if we were not living in abundance with plenty to share. Make us over in your image, and forgive us in your mercy. Amen.

## Assurance of Pardon (based on 1 Peter 2:24)

Christ himself bore our sins in his body on the cross, so that, free from sins, we might live for righteousness. By his wounds we have

April 17, 2005

been healed. In the name of Jesus Christ, we are forgiven. Glory to
God! Amen.

# Benediction

May the love of God our Protector comfort us, may the grace of
Jesus Christ our Good Shepherd cover us, and may the presence of
the Holy Spirit our Advocate fill us to overflowing. Go in peace. Go
in gratitude. Go in trust. Amen.

# Fifth Sunday of Easter

## Margaret Grun Kibben

---

**Acts 7:55-60:** Stephen faces his inevitable death with incredible joy and even fearlessness, sure of the message of salvation he has himself preached, and affirmed by the vision of the glory of God and Jesus standing at the right hand of God.

**Psalm 31:1-5, 15-16:** A psalm of extreme faith from one in extreme distress. The psalmist appeals to God's omnipotent being and steadfast love using verb images of strength and impenetrability.

**1 Peter 2:2-10:** Our sanctification in Christ is set up against the rejection we endure in our daily lives, "that [we] may proclaim the mighty acts of him who called [us] out of darkness into his marvelous light."

**John 14:1-14:** Jesus offers simple words of assurance, aware of Thomas's (and our) very human queries, and Philip's (and our) opacity. Jesus makes clear the purpose of his mission: to prepare each of us, to be the way to and to give knowledge of the Father, and to inspire our belief in him.

---

## REFLECTIONS

The serendipity that there is among these lectionary passages a common thread cannot be overlooked. This week we might put aside the tendency to focus on only one or two passages, for while each of these passages brings forth the same message of certainty and reassurance, they can build upon each other so that the message is sounded more loudly and clearly. Psalm 31, even when heard outside of its Passion Sunday context, reveals the potential for faith without sight, in fact, faith in the face of unfathomable suffering. The Gospel passage in John reveals the ultimate foundation for that faith, the words of assurance coming from the one who in fact personified the psalmist's lament.

In the early days of the church, when most of the newest followers were still sorting out the depth and breadth of the resources available to them, testing the strength of their convictions, and claiming the inheritance of Christ's authority, Stephen bursts forth with divine bravado. And as if to reassure those of us who remain behind to proclaim the good news of the gospel, yet are uncertain of our ability to live as faithfully and speak as boldly as those who have gone before us, the passage in 1 Peter offers compassion and empathy. We are reminded of our salvation in Christ, our call to this priesthood, and our identity with Christ and with the people God has mercifully chosen to proclaim the claim that God has on each of us.

# A SERMON BRIEF

My daughter watched in wonder as the man in the restaurant performed a magic trick for her. It was a fairly simple one—the old coin behind the ear trick. But written all over her face was, "How does he do that?" We, of course, looked on knowingly. It's a simple matter of *leger de main*, the slight of hand that causes these objects to slip out of sight and up a sleeve. The only problem was he wasn't wearing a sleeve. And I was reminded once again of my own wonder at his ability to perform those simple feats with such facility and confidence.

Although faith is certainly not magic, there is something supernatural about the ability some folk have to face the direst situations with the same facility and confidence in their identity with Christ, and with strength that seems simply impossible. Perhaps *supernatural* is an inappropriate term here, as it is obviously something divine rather than extraterrestrial that has bolstered their witness in the face of adversity. Even so, as I venture into Stephen's story and those of my own acquaintances, I observe with wonder and am made painfully aware of the question written on my own heart: "How do they do that?"

The chasm that exists between the despair of our everyday experience and the hope we have in Jesus Christ has never ceased to amaze me. Like that realm into which the magical coin seems to disappear, the realm of faith seems at times to be equally unknowable. The difference is that I know that magic tricks are learned, and faith is a gift of grace—and that makes it seem not only unknowable but unavailable. My heart is troubled and afraid. Like Thomas, I ask, "How can I know the way? How can I know how to 'do' faith?" Or like Philip, I want to be tutored: "Show me and I will be satisfied."

The answer Jesus gives is that faith, of course, is not "knowable" or learned behavior. When Jesus responds to the paradigmatic disciples, he thwarts all publishers' caution and uses the word *believe* four times in three sentences. No other word fits; it is simply a matter of belief. There is nothing to learn, no secret techniques, nothing even magical about faith. Believe. And in believing, only then will we too do the works of Jesus, even greater works than these. That is, we too—no matter how dire our situation, no matter how unavailable strength may seem—will exhibit the power available to each of us in Christ.

While I can think of several people in my own experience who could serve as examples to this witness, the story of Stephen provides a common reference. The fact that he hadn't exactly won the hearts and minds of the council by comparing them to their stiff-necked ancestors notwithstanding, that he understood his mission to be God's mouthpiece in the face of his certain death demonstrates an inspiration—a filling—of the Spirit of God. Consider also the psalmist in his tortured, isolated existence who speaks with confidence and assurance to the rock of his salvation, "You are my God." It is not talent that is the source of their strength but their chosenness. They belong to God, and it is God's mercy that has bolstered their confidence.

I may never learn to do a magic trick. And I must say I relish the wonder in my daughter's eyes inasmuch as it speaks to my own. But as I observe the strength and confidence of my partners in faith, I am reminded that I belong to God too; that I may proclaim God's mighty acts in my life, in their lives, and in the lives of the company of saints who have gone before us. It is belief, plain and simple, in Jesus Christ who has bridged the gap between our lives and God's plan for our redemption. Plain and simple, but no less wonder-full.

# SUGGESTIONS FOR WORSHIP

## Call to Worship (based on Psalm 31)

LEADER:     In you, O Lord, we seek refuge. Do not let us be ashamed, but in your righteousness deliver us.

PEOPLE:     **Incline your ear to us. Be a rock of refuge for us, our strong fortress.**

LEADER:      Into your hand we commit our spirits. Our times are in your hand.

PEOPLE:      **Let your face shine upon your servants; in your steadfast love may we find our salvation.**

# Prayer of Confession and Assurance of Pardon

ALL:      **Gracious God, we approach you in our blindness and our uncertainty. In Christ you have provided for us the way to you, and we have chosen our own only to find ourselves constantly distressed and in perpetual trouble. Through the witness of the saints, you have demonstrated that our faith in Christ will deliver us from all peril, and yet we tremble and falter at the slightest hint of challenge. Forgive us our willfulness, remind us again of your strength, and open our eyes to your steadfast love, that we may be emboldened to proclaim your reign over all things.**

LEADER:      But you are a chosen race, a royal priesthood, a holy nation, God's own people. Once you were no one, now in Christ you belong to God. Once you received no mercy, but now you in Christ have received mercy.

# Benediction

The God of all grace, who has called you to his eternal glory in Christ, will himself restore, support, strengthen, and establish you. To him be the power forever and ever. Amen.

# Sixth Sunday of Easter

## Lillian Daniel

---

**Acts 17:22-31:** At the Areopagus in Athens, Paul declares the "unknown god" of the Athenians to be the God who is Lord of heaven and earth.

**Psalm 66:8-20:** The psalmist praises God for safely bringing "us out to a spacious place."

**1 Peter 3:13-22:** Even those who are baptized in Jesus Christ may be called to suffer, but our baptism ensures the power and presence of God with us.

**John 14:15-21:** Jesus promises that God will send to his followers the "Advocate," who will enable them to keep Jesus' commandments.

---

## REFLECTIONS

The Gospel reading for this week includes that beautiful line from Scripture that Jesus offers to his friends toward the end of his life: "I will not leave you orphaned" (John 14:18). I have read this line at funerals and preached it on Sundays, and every time someone tells me afterward how much that one line of Scripture has meant.

Of course adoption is a pastoral concern. At any given time, there are families in the church hoping to conceive a child or considering adopting one. There are people who were orphaned and then adopted with happy or unhappy results. Others may sit in the pews and remember being shuffled from one foster home to another. Another person may remember the dad who said he would never leave, only to wake up one morning and find that he had slipped away into another life.

As the pastor, you never know the private and tender hopes people bring to church on any given morning. So Jesus reassures us, as pastors, "I will not leave you orphaned." We preach this word and allow the Holy Spirit to salve the wounds and open the mind. As Christians, we know to whom we belong, but even we need the reminder every Sunday.

The sophisticated people of Athens to whom Paul spoke in the epistle text from Acts did not know that they needed reassurance. They thought that it made sense to pray to "an unknown god." Most likely they had never heard Jesus call God "Abba," an intimate term they would have found shocking to apply to an *unknown* God. They had never heard about Paul's relationship with the living Christ. And so Paul tells them that God does not live in our human constructions or depend upon our actions, but that God means for us to find our place, just as an orphan might arrive at what finally feels like home.

# A SERMON BRIEF

## "I Will Not Leave You Orphaned"

Have you seen the articles in the last few years about adoption fairs? Apparently in a culture where everyone wants to adopt babies, there are other children who are known as "hard to place." The older children, the physically challenged, and the siblings who want to stay together just can't compete on paper with the newborn. So in a desperate attempt to find homes for these "hard to place" children, some states have resorted to adoption fairs.

Potential parents arrive at a park or a playground to spend a few hours of social time with a pool of children who need to be adopted. The adults toss Frisbees, eat hot dogs, and push the swings of children who may or may not be chosen to someday eat at their kitchen tables or keep a toothbrush in their bathrooms.

Social workers stress that this is not an audition but a way to reassure wary parents that the "hard to place" orphans are wonderful kids. There are many happy adoptions that have come out of these fairs, stories of parents and children who met and immediately knew they were meant to be together.

On the other hand, there are other stories that make us cringe, those about the children who don't get picked. There are the children who have attended adoption fairs before and worry that this fair will end as others have, with no invitation. *Will I be left orphaned?* But still they hope. After all, deep within every one of us is the hope that somewhere there is a place where we belong.

"I will not leave you orphaned," Jesus said to the disciples, to the ragtag band of followers who were getting used to having him around.

"Of course you won't leave us orphaned," someone may have replied. "This movement is really starting to build. You're here for good, right?"

But just one chapter back in the Gospel of John, we have heard, "Now before the festival of the Passover, Jesus knew that his hour had come to depart from this world and go to the Father" (13:1). Those words about a son and a father reuniting linger eerily next to his promise not to leave his earthly friends orphaned.

In going to meet his own father, Jesus knows that some people will feel abandoned, even as he will be embraced by the loving parent who gave him life. Before he goes, he prepares his friends: the loss ahead will not be the final ending that it appears to be.

"In a little while the world will no longer see me," Jesus says, adding, "but you will see me; because I live, you also will live" (14:18-19).

You will not be as alone as you feel.

You are never as alone as you feel.

"On that day, you will know that I am in my Father, and you in me, and I in you" (v. 20). Not only will you have a place, you will be in a place where there is no such thing as place. One space will bleed into another, all of us within one another, outside the bounds of this world. Imagine a world in which you are never abandoned, and where you always belong.

This section of John's Gospel is not just a word of comfort of course. Jesus always pairs comfort with critique. So just as we are basking in the vision of this holy embrace, Jesus follows his promise to love us forever with a few words about what love actually is.

Contrary to modern ideas, for Jesus, love is not a feeling. Love is not a mood or a magical spell. Love is something related to action. "They who have my commandments and keep them are those who love me" (v. 21). *I will not leave you orphaned, but once you are adopted into my family, there will be rules and expectations.*

Remember that in the time and place where Jesus spoke, the gap between the rich and the poor could mean the difference between life and death. Orphans who were not taken in truly lacked shelter. Orphans died of exposure. Becoming an orphan was not considered a psychological issue. But it might well be a death sentence. Instead, Jesus offers a way of life.

Jesus will not leave us orphaned, but we are called to a radical love in which no one is orphaned by God or by human beings. Who have we left out in the cold? Who have we left orphaned in this world of pain? As we have been embraced, whom are we called to enfold in loving and protective arms?

There is a sense of urgency to Jesus' words "If you love me, you will keep my commandments." *What will happen after I am gone? How will anyone know of God's embrace? If I leave you for just three days, what will be left of me, if you do not show my love in what you do?*

To the smugly saved who think that they owe nothing to the world around them; to the spiritually overconfident who think that they are so loved that their actions no longer matter; to the ones who love only when they feel like it, Jesus says, "They who have my commandments and keep them are those who love me."

To any child who has ever been lost in the towering canned goods aisle of a grocery store; to any grownup who has stood at an aging parent's hospital bed and wondered, *"What will become of me?"*; to anyone who has ever made so many wrong turns that the person doubts there can ever be a home he or she can return to, Jesus says, "I will not leave you orphaned." Amen.

# SUGGESTIONS FOR WORSHIP

## Call to Worship (based on Acts 17:24-28)

LEADER:    The God who made heaven and earth does not live in shrines made by human hands.

**PEOPLE:    For God gave to mortals our breath, our life, and everything.**

LEADER:    From one child, God made all the nations to inhabit the earth.

**PEOPLE:    God allotted the times of their existence and the boundaries where they live,**

LEADER:    So that people might search, and perhaps grope for God

**PEOPLE:    And then find God;**

LEADER:    For the Lord is not far from each one of us.

**PEOPLE:    In Christ we live and move and have our being.**

125

# Call to Confession

LEADER: We come before Christ's presence, hearing his words, "They who have my commandments and keep them are those who love me." Examine our hearts, O Lord, and reveal to us where we have fallen short of your divine destiny. Hear our silent confession and, in the whispers of our hearts, shout your grace. To you we offer these moments of silent prayer in the hope that when our minds are still, we will hear your word. (*Silent Prayer of Confession*)

# Assurance of Pardon
# (based on 1 Peter 3:13-16)

LEADER: Now who will harm you if you are eager to do what is good?

PEOPLE: **But even if you suffer for doing what is right, you are blessed.**

LEADER: Do not fear what others fear, and do not be intimidated,

PEOPLE: **But in your hearts sanctify Christ as Lord.**

LEADER: Always be ready to make a defense for the hope that is in you;

PEOPLE: **Yet do it with gentleness and reverence.**

LEADER: Keep your conscience clear.

PEOPLE: **For who will harm you if you are eager to do what is good?**

# Day of Pentecost

### Denise Bennett

---

**Acts 2:1-21:** The story of the Day of Pentecost among early Christian believers.

**Psalm 104:24-34, 35b:** The psalmist extols the glory of God seen in all creation.

**1 Corinthians 12:3b-13:** The varieties of gifts of the Spirit.

**John 20:19-23:** The risen Jesus breathes the Holy Spirit upon the gathered disciples.

---

## REFLECTIONS

We never celebrated Pentecost in church when I was kid growing up in the Midwest and South, so it was only after I was an adult, had left the church, and returned to churches now experiencing liturgical renewal that I was introduced to Pentecost. I think it is my favorite day in the church year. The imagery is rich in the Scriptures for this day. We find in the Acts text fire and wind; in the Gospel of John Jesus breathing the Spirit into his fearful disciples like a midwife breathing life into a newborn babe; and in Psalm 104 the Spirit giving life to all creatures, including the creepy crawlies and leviathan sporting in the sea. Pentecost reminds us that the Spirit is present, moving in our hearts and lives, *inspiring* us to worship, work, and live more creatively together as the body of Christ; *firing* us to imagine alternatives to the "same old, same old" of sin and death.

Some of the best worship I have experienced on Pentecost employed liturgical dance, red banners blown by unseen fans, and even bowls of fire. Why not celebrate? It is after all the birthday of the church. I worship with a lively group of college students and people from the greater community who are willing to try new things in worship. This poem/story/sermon for leader and congregation is for them. It came to me all as one piece, spilling out onto the computer keys like new wine breaking out of old wineskins. I hear it with walking bass and drums, a cool jazz version of the story of how the Spirit made the disciples red-hot to tell the good news to the world.

# A SERMON BRIEF

Pentecost has been called the birthday of the church. On that morning the Spirit came and gifted all the followers of Jesus, not just the leaders, to speak the truth of God's power and love into the world. Men and women, young and old, received the Spirit that morning, and later it would be both Jews and Gentiles, slaves and free people, who would also be set on fire to tell the good news of the coming of the kingdom to anyone who would listen. As we heard in the passage from 1 Corinthians 12, the Spirit graces us in many different ways; and though the gifts may vary from person to person, they all come from the same Spirit. The gifts of the Spirit are given for "the common good," as Paul says, to nurture and nourish the body of Christ, the church.

Pentecost celebrates communication—everyone can understand what the Spirit is saying—and it celebrates community. All the people preach. So in that Spirit I invite you to join with me in telling the Pentecost story. This version of the story is told with a jazzy rhythm because jazz reminds me so much of the work of the Spirit. In jazz improvisation, the players are inspired to move beyond the safety of the notes on the page to play the same tune in a new way. And while some jazz might sound like "every man or woman for himself or herself," the best jazz, in my opinion, happens when the players improvise but still play together in the same key. And so the Spirit inspires us to move beyond the safety of our old patterns, those same tunes we've played so many times in the same way, to improvise. The Spirit inspires us to play the old song of God's love in a new way that all might understand; not to show our virtuosity, but to allow the Spirit to play through us in the same key. (Here I give directions for reading the story together, with the congregation reading the lines in bold italics.)

We were gathered that morning in the upper room
***We were waiting, we were waiting***

With our sisters and brothers in Jerusalem
*We were waiting, we were waiting*
Jesus had said the Holy Spirit would come
*We were waiting, we were waiting*
To give us power and loosen our tongues
*We were waiting, we were waiting*

Pentecost morning dawned clear and bright
*We were praying, we were praying*
And we gathered to pray in the morning light
*We were praying, we were praying*
When out of the quiet there came a sound
*We were praying, we were praying*
A rushing wind began to pound
*We were praying, we were praying*
It filled the house, it filled our souls
*We were praying, we were praying*
A breath of life, like a midwife blows
*We were praying, we were praying*
A rush of joy, like the waters of birth
*We were praying, we were praying*
The Spirit laboring on the earth
*We were praying, we were praying*
Tongues of fire haloing each
*We were praying, we were praying*

Our hearts aflame, we began to preach
*We were preaching, we were preaching*
In languages from far and near,
*We were preaching, we were preaching*
Praising God whose love casts out fear
*We were preaching, we were preaching*
Love like that can't sit and hide
*We were preaching, we were preaching*
It spilled out of the house to the crowd outside
*We were preaching, we were preaching*
All who heard were quite amazed,
*We were preaching, we were preaching*
In their own languages to hear God praised
*We were preaching, we were preaching*
They came from Parthia, Pontus, Egypt, Arabia

*We were preaching, we were preaching*
Crete, and Cyrene, Libya, Asia
*We were preaching, we were preaching*
In Cappadocia, and Phrygia they made their homes,
*We were preaching, we were preaching*
And don't forget Elam and Rome,
*We were preaching, we were preaching*
And a few other places I can't pronounce
*We were preaching, we were preaching*
But all understood God's power announced
*We were preaching, we were preaching*
But others laughed, "They're full of new wine!"
*We were preaching, we were preaching*
It's easy to "dis" what you can't define
*We were preaching, we were preaching*
We were full of new wine, but not the kind they meant
*We were preaching, we were preaching*
It was the wine of the Spirit, it was Heaven sent
*We were preaching, we were preaching*

By wind and fire on Pentecost morn
*We are the body, we are the body*
The body of Christ, the church was born
*We are the body, we are the body*
Two thousand years later we gather still
*We are the body, we are the body*
To pray and preach, to teach and heal
*We are the body, we are the body*
To be that love that casts out fear
*We are the body, we are the body*
But we need the Spirit, that's oh so clear!
*We are the body, we are the body*
For without the Spirit, we are only dust,
*We are the body, we are the body*
Creator, sustainer, in you we trust
*We are the body, we are the body*
Come Holy Spirit, come quickening breath
*We are the body, we are the body*
Raise us again to life from death.
*We are the body, we are the body*
Renew us, remake us, fire us, shake us

*We are the body, we are the body*
From the slumber of sin, come, wake us
*We are the body, we are the body*
Let us see with your eyes; let us touch with your hands
*We are the body, we are the body*
Speak only your love, and let all understand.
*We are the body, we are the body*
*We are the body, we are the body*
*We are the body of Christ. Amen!*

# SUGGESTIONS FOR WORSHIP

## Call to Worship

ONE:      We are all gathered in one place, waiting . . .
MANY:      **Come, Holy Spirit!**
ONE:      Scared, tired, or maybe even bored, still we are waiting . . .
MANY:      **Come, Holy Spirit!**
ONE:      Breathe life into us, fire our hearts, loosen our tongues to praise you!
ALL:      **Come, Holy Spirit!**

## Prayer of Confession

You offer us the breath of life, O God, but we turn away. You offer to free us from the bondage of fear, but we prefer the familiar. You have work for us to do, but we keep our own agendas. You offer us dreams and visions, voices to witness and pray with, but we refuse your gifts. Forgive us for trying to quench the Spirit. Give us courage to accept the challenges your gifts bring. Amen.

## Assurance of Pardon

ONE:      When they were frightened and in despair, Jesus appeared among his disciples, offering them peace and breathing into them the new life of the Spirit. So he comes to us, offering forgiveness and new life in him. Friends, you are loved and forgiven. Be at peace.
MANY:      **You are loved and forgiven. Be at peace. Amen.**

# Ordinary Time 15 or Proper 10

## M. Jan Holton

---

**Genesis 25:19-34:** The story of Esau and Jacob, the sons of Isaac.

**Psalm 119:105-112:** God's word is a "lamp to my feet and a light to my path."

**Romans 8:1-11:** A description of life in the Spirit.

**Matthew 13:1-9, 18-23:** The parable of the sower.

---

## REFLECTIONS

The Old Testament lesson is the starting point for the wonderfully rich story of Jacob and Esau. The text, particularly verses 29-34, prepares the reader for the more elaborate and ultimately divisive conflict that occurs later in the story when Jacob steals his elder brother's blessing from the aging Isaac. This blessing is the glue that holds together the inheritance. Once it is given it cannot be rescinded.

Many of us have read this scripture passage so often that it is probably very familiar. By habit, I usually turn first to examine Jacob's behavior. But what about Esau? Is he the victim in this encounter? It is striking to me how utterly careless Esau is in regard to his birthright. He discards the blessing of his birth as aimlessly as one sheds a pair of dirty socks at the end of a long day.

As Christians, we have come to understand that we too share in a *birthright*. That birthright is hope, the hope of the gospel. After reading of the encounter between Jacob and Esau, we may see reflections of our own behavior. How often do we also carelessly disregard God's blessings? Our lives can become so distorted that it becomes difficult to even recognize God's blessings. At other times we simply forget to look.

This brief foray into the struggle between these two brothers reminds us of the messiness of the human struggle for faithfulness.

Likewise, it cautions us against claiming too quickly that we are victims of God's betrayal. Rather, we are reminded of our own accountability, even responsibility, for keeping our hearts open to receiving God's blessing.

# A SERMON BRIEF

## "A Birthright of Hope"

I quit smoking several years ago. The first few weeks I spent much of my time rearranging the furniture in my home. By making these familiar spaces feel different I hoped to fool my addiction into releasing me of the immediate need for a cigarette every time I sat in my favorite chair. Week by week I traveled around the room, each time viewing it from a slightly different perspective. Even small changes in the position from which we view familiar things can make them suddenly new and different.

When we engage a story as familiar to us as this one of Jacob and Esau, we may need to "rearrange the furniture" a bit in order to find a new perspective from which to view it. If viewed from Esau's corner, for example, one may quickly notice a striking shift of focus in this story. No longer are we most immediately struck by the swindling Jacob who connives to steal his brother's birthright. Rather, we find an arrogant and careless Esau who so disregards the promise and blessing of his birthright that he squanders it on a plate of stew.

Beginning with Esau's birth, we are gently persuaded to notice the connection of this child with the rich ruddy color of the soil. The repetition of the word for red in the Hebrew text ("give me some from the red red stuff") easily, and I think intentionally, draws the reader's attention to the earthiness of this encounter. Perhaps the author is also using this red earthiness to draw our attention momentarily into the past and the blood-soaked ground upon which Abel dies at the hands of Cain. Although here Esau aimlessly discards the blessing rather than claim it as his own. His only desire is to meet his immediate physical needs. This carelessness is matched only by the greed of a younger brother always at the ready to take advantage of any situation from which he can benefit. Yes, indeed, this story is a wonderful example of the *earthy* messiness that we have come to expect from the book of Genesis.

Such messiness should make us feel right at home. How careless we, too, can become with God's promise even when we are sure that

133

the roots of that promise run deep into our soul. Like the eldest son, Esau, we also are heirs to a promise: God's promise through Jesus Christ. Even at the great cost of his life upon the cross, Christ calls us into blessing and bestows hope upon us as a kind of "birthright." Yet how easy it is for some of us to overlook the presence of God's promise and the blessings that promise holds. When we do so, hope is in jeopardy. Like Esau who can only hear the grumbling of his belly, we may find ourselves distracted by the sometimes-taxing burden of meeting our physical needs. But, true to the tradition of excess for which our culture has become famous, we can become equally distracted by the apathy of a life that has grown too comfortable. We have become so careless with God's blessings that we often do not recognize them when they are right in front of us.

The hurricane season of 1998 was a disastrous one for Nicaragua. Hurricane Mitch wrought such havoc on this already poor nation that officials estimated it will take thirty years to regain financial ground. As a relief worker, I was overwhelmed by the vastness of the destruction. Everything within sight was awash with the reddish brown color of the earth that the rains had washed down the mountains.

My companion and I arrived at a small village deep in the countryside to deliver relief supplies, the first the residents had seen. Small shacks had been constructed from stray pieces of wood and then covered by black construction plastic. Several deep holes stood in the middle of the makeshift village. Only then, three months after the hurricane, had they found the resources to dig latrines and construct the shaky structures they would call home. Their only source of water was the chocolate brown river that flowed nearby. The children all seemed to have colds and coughs. Some were injured. There were no doctors or medicine available. The people had no food.

Not long after we arrived, I felt a colleague pulling excitedly at my arm. She led me past a small fire heating a thin dark stew and into the small makeshift tent that was home to a family of eight. There, lying on some blankets, was the newest member of the family born only seven days before. Instead of feeling joy, my heart broke. The very tiny child was wearing a pink dress, her only one I am sure, and a small red winter knit cap. She wore no diapers. I looked at the tiny face and pink skin. She was so fragile. "So young to have nothing," my companion said. I did not expect that the child would survive these conditions for very long. With little warning one of the workers took the baby, now in her mother's arms, and placed her into mine. When the infant looked up to me, I am sorry to say, she did not find eyes that reflected a heart of faith or the assurance of God's promise. Instead, she found eyes filled with anger because of the suffering of such a small child. I looked around for her mother, who I was sure shared my indignation. Her response startled me. She was not angry. Not only was she smiling, she was beaming. This young mother understood what neither Esau nor I could grasp: the precious nature of our birthright as children of God—hope. In my mind, hope centered upon the practicalities of living: food for the hungry, medicine for the sick, and comfort for the grieving. Yet for that mother there was hope even without food, medicine, or shelter. I was holding in my arms the very promise of God to be present in the life of this woman. That mother knew better than I the risk to her child's life under these conditions. But she also knew that, whatever happens tomorrow, this day the promise of God was with her. And this promise held enough hope for that one day. Even should her daughter die, God's promise would live. It was enough. The mother would not forsake it.

Will we dare to face each day with the same faith in God's promise? Will we accept the blessing?

# SUGGESTIONS FOR WORSHIP

## Opening Prayer
## (based on Matthew 13:1-9, 18-23)

We come before you this day, God, hungry for your word. Prepare our hearts like the deep rich soil into which the sower plants the seeds. Relieve the weight of the heavy burdens we carry like stones within us. Turn them over, move them to the side as would the sower tilling the ground. Relieve us of the thorny anger to which we have held tight lest it choke us like a wild vine. Bless us, God, with joy as we receive your word and as we worship and praise you. May your love and understanding nurture us as we prepare to be your disciples. Amen.

## Prayer of Confession and Assurance of Pardon

ONE:        Let us together confess our sin before God and one another.

ALL: Gracious and ever-patient God, we have too often walked unaware past the blessings you have offered into our days and our lives. We have been too busy or too tired to answer when you have called. We have failed to be your blessing to others, ignoring their needs in favor of our own. Forgive us, Lord, that we have distorted your hope for justice and peace, and instead have settled for what is easy and comfortable. Renew in us, O God, faithful hearts and ready eyes so that we may recognize and rejoice at the signs of your grace at work in our lives and in the world.

ONE: In the name of Jesus Christ, go forth in the assurance that you are forgiven.

# Benediction

Go forth in peace. Remember and rejoice in God's promise for you. Open your hearts to receive the blessings that come before you each day. In gratitude, and with love and grace as your strength, may you go forth to bring hope to others and to the world. In the name of our Lord Jesus Christ. Amen.

# Ordinary Time 22 or Proper 17

Beverly A. Zink-Sawyer

---

**Exodus 3:1-15:** Moses hears the voice of God from a burning bush and receives the divine name and his own commission.

**Psalm 105:1-6, 23-26, 45c:** The psalmist praises God's "deeds among the peoples."

**Romans 12:9-21:** The writer to the Romans lists the marks of the true Christian.

**Matthew 16:21-28:** Jesus foretells his death and resurrection and bids his disciples to "take up their cross and follow me."

---

## REFLECTIONS

The metaphor of *journey* is often used to describe the Christian life. It implies the realization that we are always, it is hoped, moving from what we are to what Christ would have us be, while living with the grace-full acknowledgment that we may never quite reach the goals set before us.

*Journey* is an appropriate metaphor for people who claim their heritage within the Judeo-Christian tradition. The Old Testament is replete with examples of journeys: Abram setting out for Canaan at the command of God; Moses heeding the call of "I AM" from the core of a burning bush; the people of Israel forced to journey from their homeland into exile, then allowed to journey back home to new life.

There are yet more journeys to be made in response to the Messiah's coming: the journey of Mary and Joseph to Bethlehem; the journey of the Magi to greet the holy child; the journeys of faithful Anna and Simeon to declare God's redemptive plan in the child Jesus; and later the journey of a man named Saul, whose life—and consequently the life of the first-century world and all worlds to come—is changed along the way.

But the defining journey in all of Christian history is the journey of Jesus to Jerusalem to fulfill God's promise of salvation. Today's Gospel text is Matthew's version of that critical turning point in Jesus' inevitable journey to the cross. Here Jesus specifically addresses the disciples, those who had already embarked upon dangerous journeys of faith in response to Jesus' call, to level with them concerning just what a rocky, rough journey it would be for all of them. Given the bleakness of Jesus' prediction, it's no wonder Peter speaks for all of us in expressing incredulity at this unwelcome news.

This journey, as we know, would not have a happy ending—at least not in the short run. Jesus knew that when he turned from the crowds to confront the disciples. Matthew's first-century community under siege knew that. Countless martyrs and witnesses to the truth of Christian faith have known that. And yet they followed faithfully where Jesus led, holding fast to the promise that one day the Son of Man will come with his angels in the glory of God. Now we are called to do the same.

# A SERMON BRIEF

## "Saying 'I Do' All Over Again"

It's that time of year again—the last chance of the summer to pack the suitcases, load the car, and head off to exotic places. In our peripatetic culture, it's considered a sacrilege not to travel somewhere for summer vacation. And so, while we are still doing laundry from the last journey, we are planning the next. We decide on the perfect location, make the requisite visit to the "Triple A" office to collect our maps and tour books, pack some comfortable shoes and sunscreen, fill up the gas tank, and head off. As humorist Erma Bombeck once observed, summer vacations in America are such an art form that most of us go about planning our journeys as if we were planning the invasion of Normandy.

Maybe that's why the idea of the Christian journey scares us. We're not sure how to pack. We don't know which roadmaps to take along. Because we don't know where we're going—a realization that terrifies those of us who like to plan ahead. Throughout the Gospels, Jesus calls would-be disciples to leave what they are doing and follow him. James and John dropped their fishing nets. Matthew put down his pen and closed the tax books. And they got up to follow Jesus. But Jesus doesn't tell them where they're going. At first it isn't so difficult.

They hear some intriguing teachings. They see some miracles. They have a few skirmishes with the scribes and Pharisees.

But then the other shoe drops. Jesus' words take on a new edge, a new sense of urgency, as Matthew's Gospel account unfolds. His words to his disciples became more cryptic—and more ominous. "Jesus began to show his disciples that he must go to Jerusalem and undergo great suffering . . . and be killed. . . ." "If any want to become my followers, let them deny themselves and take up their cross and follow me."

It's a strange time of year for this text to appear in the lectionary. It seems more suited for the beginning of Lent when we re-create Jesus' journey to Jerusalem. But here we are at the end of summer, in the middle of the long season of the church year known as "Ordinary Time." We go on for weeks after Pentecost, being lulled into complacent Christianity with familiar Bible stories and nice moralisms from Paul. And then, Wham! We are hit with one of the most difficult—and pivotal—texts of the entire New Testament.

But on second thought, maybe this is the best time of the year to consider this text. Maybe we need to hear it when we least expect it, for it serves as a reminder that Christian discipleship is not something we think about once a year. The cost of holding on to a vision of the kingdom of God when everyone around us is blinded by despair hits us in the face every day. And every day we are challenged to renew our commitment to follow Jesus.

Some years ago before I was married, I read an article by a marriage counselor who made the point that couples don't say "I do" just one day of their lives. Instead, even the strongest of marriages demand that spouses say "I do" again and again and again as they live out the realities of life together. I found that idea interesting, but it didn't mean a whole lot to me—until I got married myself. And now I realize how true that writer's words are; how essential it is to remember every day the commitment made years ago to be a loving and faithful spouse. It's a commitment that doesn't mean much until you experience the joys and sorrows, the plenty and want, the sickness and health, that mark the seasons of life.

The same is true of saying "I do" to following Jesus. You probably know the old gospel hymn that talks about following Jesus with no turning back. Well, that's the ideal: setting off on the road to Jerusalem and not looking back. But it's not that easy, for there are roadblocks along the way that make us want to take another path. There are compelling sights and sounds that would lure us back to a way of life that is defined by comfort and success. There are responsibilities that, yes, we believe God has placed upon us: jobs to do, children and parents to care for, churches to run, and communities to serve.

Thanks be to God there have been those who stayed on the road to Jerusalem and have left for us their examples of faith. There have been prophets and martyrs, brave men and women who picked up their crosses and followed Jesus, leaving their own needs and desires behind because it was the faithful thing to do. We can name those saints, from Paul and Peter and Perpetua of the early church, to modern-day saints like Mother Teresa, who exemplified discipleship in its purest form. But you probably have your own canon of saints, people who managed to bear unbearable burdens with faith and courage because they promised to follow Jesus; people who lovingly care for dying spouses and handicapped children, who never abandoned a prodigal son, who wouldn't miss a week volunteering at the nursing home, who give from what little they have to fund scholarships and soup kitchens. Because of their examples, we know that maybe, just maybe, we too can follow the way of Jesus.

So we set our faces toward Jerusalem, pick up our crosses, and say "I do" all over again—"I do" to following Jesus. No, we don't know where he will lead us, or what potholes and detours we might encounter on the way. But what we *do* know is that we walk not alone, but in the company of those who have walked this way before us, even our risen Lord himself. May God grant us grace and strength for the journey.

# SUGGESTIONS FOR WORSHIP

## Call to Worship (based on Psalm 105)

LEADER:    O give thanks to the Lord, call on the name of the Lord.

**PEOPLE:**    **Make known God's deeds among all the peoples.**

LEADER:    Sing to the Lord; sing praises to the name of the Lord.

**PEOPLE:**    **Let the hearts of those who seek the Lord rejoice.**

## Prayer of Confession

You call us, O Lord, as you have called your servants for all the generations of your people on earth. Forgive us when we are slow to answer, when we are paralyzed by fear and doubt. Give us courage to follow in the footsteps of the faithful who have gone before us, trusting your faithfulness and proclaiming your truth. Through Jesus Christ our Lord.

# Benediction (based on Romans 12)

And now go out into the world in peace. Let love be genuine, hate what is evil, and hold fast to what is good. Rejoice in hope, be patient in suffering, and persevere in prayer. Do not be overcome by evil, but overcome evil with good. Love and serve the Lord, rejoicing in the power of the Holy Spirit. Amen.

# Ordinary Time 28 or Proper 23

Vicki G. Lumpkin

---

**Isaiah 25:1-9:** The prophet anticipates the day of God's deliverance.

**Psalm 23:** The shepherd psalm.

**Philippians 4:1-9:** Paul urges the Colossian believers to rejoice, forgo worry, and live in the certainty of God's peace in Jesus Christ.

**Matthew 22:1-14:** Jesus tells the parable of the wedding banquet.

---

## REFLECTIONS

The Old Testament texts, in concert with the Gospel reading, portray visions of a gracious and inclusive God who provides a banquet for God's own. Also included in this picture is the specter of judgment; God's enemies are excluded from the feast. The tension between invitation/inclusion and judgment/exclusion is maintained in the parable of the wedding banquet.

The Gospel text occurs in the context of Jesus' last week of ministry. The chief priests and the elders accosted him in the temple and demanded that he tell on whose authority he was teaching (Matthew 21:23). In response, he told three parables. The text for today is the final one of the series. The passage is noteworthy for its depiction of God's gracious and sweeping invitation; the slaves of the king are instructed to go out and invite "everyone." The parable also depicts a two-fold judgment, first on the invited guests and then on the one who entered without the proper clothing. As such, it speaks not only to the original questioners, but also to Matthew's audience and to us.

The parable begs several questions: What is the nature of the invitation? What does it mean to accept? What is appropriate clothing? Where are such garments to be found? How does one put them on? What does it mean to say that "many are called, but few are chosen"?

# A SERMON BRIEF

## "Dressed for the Party"

"Fashion statement," "dressed for success," "best dressed list," "clothes make the man" (and the woman, too!), "dressed up," "dressed down"—our language is full of images about the way we are clothed. Color, fabric, cut and style, the unofficial uniform of the preadolescent or the power suit of the workplace, what we choose to wear says something about what we do, how we see ourselves, or how we want others to see us. So it is no surprise that from the fig leaf of Genesis to the white robes of Revelation, from Joseph's robe of many colors to the garment of Jesus for which the Roman soldiers cast lots, the Bible too speaks about clothing. That is true of the Gospel passage for today as well.

Matthew records that Jesus told this story, the parable of the wedding feast, during the last days of his earthly ministry. It was told in response to questions from the chief priests and elders. As he taught in the temple, they challenged him: "Tell us on whose authority you are doing these things." In reply, he told them three parables; this is the final one. The parable is important because it tells us something about God, what God is like and what God expects. It also tells us something about ourselves. For the listeners, then and now, it is both a parable of hope and a parable of judgment.

The story offers a message of hope because of the radical inclusiveness of the offer. The invitation to the party that was first sent to a few is now presented to all of us. There are no restrictions. No matter which highway or byway we find ourselves on, no matter what marketplace we're working in, whether we're rich or poor, powerful or not, "evil or good," there is a place at the table for you and me.

The parable also speaks of the awesome freedom that God has given us. We have been given an invitation, a choice, to come to the party, to be in fellowship with God. The text tells us up front that not everyone will accept; some will be too wrapped up in their own affairs to bother, but no one is forced to come. There are serious consequences for rejection, that is part of the judgment inherent in the story; but the option of saying no is a real one. Then of course there is also the issue of what to wear.

My husband and I were married during the closing years of the Vietnam War. The draft was still in effect and, barring some compelling reason, if you had a low number, you were going to be called into service. After he finished college, my husband went into the Army. I remember him coming home on one of his first days of training with an armload of clothing. There were dress uniforms and work uniforms, combat boots and dress shoes, and a variety of hats, all in olive green. The "uniform of the day" was selected by someone higher up and was based on the season, the location, and the job to be done. Sometimes there was a choice—a person could wear a short jacket instead of a long one—but the options were always limited and always prescribed by someone else.

Just like members of the military services, the parable of the wedding feast suggests that those who reside in the commonwealth of God can be distinguished by how they're clothed. There is a certain uniform worn by the people of God. The uniform is not distinguished by the cut or fabric of people's clothing—that has varied mightily over the course of the last two millennia—but by matters of style. There is a pattern that we are expected to conform to. To wear the uniform or not is our choice, but the look, the style, of the uniform is not. That is up to God.

In order to remain at the party, we are obliged to take off our old lifestyle and to put on a "uniform of grace" that is characterized by the love of God. This is a way of clothing our hearts and minds that bespeaks a new status and a new role. We are now the children of God, and we are expected to act like it. We are expected to take on—to put on—the character of our older Brother and our heavenly Parent. That is the uniform, the wedding robe, God expects to see on us.

Where are such garments to be found? How does one put them on? Just as the invitation to the party comes from God, so does the clothing of grace. It is a creation of God that is designed and manufactured by Godself. It is God's work that is effected within our willing hearts and minds. To put on such garments requires two things: saying yes, and accepting the ongoing process of transformation—of being *conformed* to the image of Christ, of being *transformed* "by the renewing of our minds" and hearts.

So it is that the text tells us that "many are called, but few are chosen." What does that mean? I think it means that there are those who hear the call of God, who get the invitation, but who refuse to take it seriously. They come for the party but refuse to stay for the cleanup afterward. They want the benefits of the commonwealth but not the obligations. Make no mistake about it, there are obligations. There is a tension, a paradox, in the parable, because while it tells us that everyone is invited, it also tells us that not every response to the invitation is acceptable. That is also part of the judgment inherent in the story.

The parable of the wedding feast offers both good news and bad. The good news is that there's a party, and you're invited. The bad news, if one considers it such, is that there's a dress requirement. Oh! One more thing—has God got an awesome wardrobe for you!

# SUGGESTIONS FOR WORSHIP

## Call to Worship

ONE:        Go into the highways and byways,
ALL:        **Into the main streets and the marketplace.**
ONE:        The ox and the fatted calves have been killed.
ALL:        **The feast is ready.**
ONE:        Invite them all!
ALL:        **Come, rich and poor!**
ONE:        Come, beggar and tax collector!
ALL:        **Come to the banquet of our God!**

## Prayer of Confession

God of grace, we confess that we often fail to take seriously your call to live a life that reflects your touch. Instead of living in harmony, we are in turmoil with ourselves and with each other. Instead of being gentle, we are harsh. Instead of rejoicing, we criticize. Instead of trusting you, we worry. Restore our spirits that our lives might give evidence of your presence within and among us. In Christ's name. Amen.

## Assurance of Pardon

ONE:        The words of Isaiah promise: "The Lord GOD will wipe away the tears from all faces, and the disgrace of the people will be taken away from all the earth, for the LORD has spoken" (25:8 adapted).

ALL: **Thanks be to God, for we are forgiven.**

# Benediction

Clothe yourselves in garments of love, truth, peace, and justice; and return to your homes dressed for the heavenly banquet. Go with the assurance that such finery will never wear out, go out of shape, or out of style. Go in the knowledge that this is the raiment of God, the fruit of transformed lives, the hope of a seeking world.

# All Saints Day

### Barbara J. MacHaffie

---

**Revelation 7:9-17:** A hymn of praise is raised by the multitude before God and before the Lamb.

**Psalm 34:1-10, 22:** The psalmist finds refuge and deliverance in the Lord.

**1 John 3:1-3:** We are called God's children as a sign of God's love.

**Matthew 5:1-12:** Jesus pronounces the Beatitudes from a mountain gathering with his disciples.

---

## REFLECTIONS

Revelation 7:9-17 is part of an interlude in John's description of events that will accompany the end of history. Six seals have been broken, and we wait with anticipation for the breaking of the seventh along with resurrection and judgment. What commands our attention, however, instead of the anticipated end is the church. It is a church besieged by government and culture, but also a church that is the locus of God's saving activity. Possibly to reassure those frightened and marginalized Christians of the first century, John's vision of the church is a grand one. The first part of the seventh chapter shows us the church militant, where Christians prepare to struggle against the principalities of this world and are called to yield even their lives. The second part of the chapter reveals the church triumphant after the ordeal is over.

This is a text replete with images of grandeur such as thrones and palms, songs and amens. Yet the text ends with an image that is one of the most compassionate and intimate in the biblical record. It offers a stark contrast to the spectacular gathering of the white-robed multitude. Of the faithful gathered together John writes, "God will wipe away every tear from their eyes" (v. 17). In John's words we find a reminder about the nature of God, and a possible clue for Christian living.

# A SERMON BRIEF

## "The Wounded Healer"

One of my earliest memories is being in a department store with my mother one wintry day. While she negotiated a purchase at the counter, I wandered off, mistakenly following a woman wearing a red coat similar to that worn by my mother. Panic, tears, and a quick reunion followed, and I remember clearly the way in which my mother stooped down, wiped my eyes and my nose. Revelation 7:17 brings to mind the many times my tears have been wiped, but there are few other occasions I recall so vividly. While all parents dry tears, it strikes me as a particularly maternal act that might draw us to think again about the language we use to talk about the Holy. God is warrior and king throughout the Bible, but lying as hidden treasure waiting for discovery are some other images of God—God who cries out in labor and who teaches a child to walk. And here in this sometimes alien collection of apocalyptic visions is a God who wipes away tears.

For the past several years I have had my students in an introduction to religion course read Harold Kushner's book *When Bad Things Happen to Good People*. Every summer I think about replacing it with something else. Kushner argues that God is not omnipotent and that bad things happen to people because of natural law and bad human choices. God's role in suffering, he claims, is to comfort and stand alongside of us in our pain. The argument is fraught with theological problems, yet young undergraduates eagerly embrace his work; and I am moved and stunned by their comments. Many tell me that they have never thought of God in terms other than judgment and raw creative power. Yet Kushner challenges them to think about a God who wipes away human tears, who provides strength and courage and the grace to help us remember what remains rather than what we have lost.

But there is something else in this end of history image of God that might help us better grasp holy living. For Kushner, the God who wipes away tears inspires us to reach out to people who have been hurt by life. Those who feel lonely and abandoned and judged will be comforted not only by God but by those who seek to live in God's light. And therein lies a task that is profoundly difficult. We all share similar feelings in our culture when confronted directly with the tears of another. We worry about not doing or saying the right thing. We are embarrassed because we inhabit a cultural fantasyland of perpetual success. We are angry because the messiness of life imposes itself upon us. And so we avert our eyes. We turn away and busy ourselves with something else.

Yet John tries to rescue us from our discomfort by giving us this wonderful vision of God who, in the midst of spectacular glory, stoops to wipe away tears. So this vision also becomes a clue for how we might live our lives. It reminds us that small gestures mean much when people are in pain. There is so much going on in this scene that is grand and monumental, yet God the Creator and God the Redeemer takes time out to wipe the eyes of the suffering. It also reminds us that pain and tears need to be acknowledged and confronted directly. You cannot wipe away tears without looking into the face of a person who is crying. This vision suggests that because we acknowledge pain and offer comfort, we are not then required to solve everything and make everything all right. God wipes tears for the last time when redemption is complete. We wipe tears in the "in-between" time when this is not a final act but only a temporary resolution. We can give those in sorrow a chance to breathe and see more clearly once the tears have dried. And we can offer at least a moment of serenity and dignity when the future can be pondered, however hesitantly.

One of the most remarkable stories of congregational life to appear in the last few years is Samuel Freedman's book *Upon This Rock*. Saint Paul Community Baptist Church is in one of the most desperate slums in America, yet the congregation takes enormous pride in its choirs and dance troupes, its Bible classes and business ventures. But it is the Wounded Healers who make the promise of Revelation 7:17 come alive. Freedman describes in detail those who meet in the chapel each week to overcome their addictions to drugs and alcohol. They come each Saturday in silks and sweats, sneakers and Gucci loafers—but they all wear the same Wounded Healer button. On it is a teardrop, and inside the teardrop are two people, arms outstretched, reaching toward each other. During their meetings, those present give voice to their fears and anger, their failures and successes, and they offer to each other small, practical, and godly gestures of compassion. They keep an eye open for employment for the jobless and hold spending money for those who are too unsure to trust themselves.

149

But they also hand tissue to each other, wipe each other's eyes, and hold each other's hands. In the midst of one meeting, a leader prays aloud, "We come with our ears open and our eyes wet. . . . We pray for you to come to us, God, and we ask You to be gentle."[1]

And John of Revelation might say, "Amen."

# SUGGESTIONS FOR WORSHIP

## Call to Worship (based on Matthew 5:3-8)

LEADER: Blessed are the poor in spirit, for theirs is the kingdom of heaven.

**PEOPLE: Blessed are those who mourn, for they will be comforted.**

LEADER: Blessed are the meek, for they will inherit the earth.

**PEOPLE: Blessed are those who hunger and thirst for righteousness, for they will be filled.**

LEADER: Blessed are the merciful, for they will receive mercy.

**PEOPLE: Blessed are the pure in heart, for they will see God.**

## Opening Prayer

O God, our Creator and Redeemer, whose care embraces the great and the small, look upon us and upon the world you have made with compassion. Through your grace, you seek to redeem what is lost and restore it to wholeness. You sent your son, Jesus Christ, as a Wounded Healer to repair our brokenness and dry our tears of despair. Open our hearts to Christ's healing and peace that we may be made whole and inspired to love in his name. Amen.

## Benediction

Go now into the world, rejoicing in the promise of God who reaches down to dry our tears, the power of Jesus Christ who redeems us, and the presence of the Spirit who leads us into service. Amen.

1. Samuel G. Freedman, *Upon This Rock: The Miracles of a Black Church* (New York: HarperCollins, 1993), 128.

# Christ the King (or Reign of Christ)

Martha L. Moore-Keish

---

**Ezekiel 34:11-16, 20-24:** God, the good shepherd, will care for the sheep.

**Psalm 100:** "Make a joyful noise to the Lord, all the earth!"

**Ephesians 1:15-23:** A prayer of thanksgiving for the Ephesians affirms the ascension and rule of Christ.

**Matthew 25:31-46:** Final judgment will be rendered based on the treatment of "the least of these."

---

## REFLECTIONS

On this last Sunday of the liturgical year, we celebrate Christ's reign over all earthly powers. This theme appears most clearly in the Ephesians passage. The Ezekiel passage presents another king, the good shepherd who feeds the sheep. Matthew presents Christ enthroned as judge, separating the sheep from the goats at the end of time. Most intriguing on this day is the juxtaposition of the kingly imagery with the attention to "the least of these" in Matthew. Christ's kingship is not that of domination, but of compassion for the forgotten ones. This is consistent with the picture of God as the good shepherd caring for the weak sheep in Ezekiel.

The image of judgment is uncomfortable today. We seldom think of Jesus as judge. But how much worse would it be to live in a cosmos in which God did not care about how the poorest ones are treated? This is only uncomfortable for those of us who do not identify with "the least of these."

# A SERMON BRIEF

On this last Sunday of the liturgical year, we do an odd thing in a democratic society: we celebrate Christ as King. With the writer of Ephesians, we proclaim that God raised Christ "from the dead and seated him at his right hand in the heavenly places, far above all rule and authority and power and dominion, and above every name that is named" (vv. 20-21). Matthew presents a similar image: "When the Son of Man comes in his glory, and all the angels with him, then he will sit on the throne of his glory" (v. 31). As if this language of kingship were not bad enough, Matthew presents Christ as judge, separating sheep from goats, welcoming some into blessedness, while casting others into darkness. This offends our tolerant American selves. How can we worship a king who chooses some and not others? Who is this judgmental Christ? "Who is this King of glory?" (Psalm 24:10).

We have seen him before. Do you remember? Nearly a year ago we celebrated the day when three kings saw a star in the east, and they packed up their camels and followed, convinced that it would lead them to another newborn king. Along the way, according to the opera *Amahl and the Night Visitors,* they seek shelter in a shepherd's hut. Living there are a widow and her son Amahl. Amahl and his mother welcome the kings and wonder at the beautiful gifts they are carrying. When the mother asks whom they are seeking, one king responds:

Have you seen a child the color of wheat, the color of dawn?
His eyes are mild, his hands are those of a king, as king he was born.

This child "the color of dawn," Jesus Christ, was born a king, and three other kings bring him gifts. As king, however, he was not born in any palace, but in a rough animal shelter even poorer than the shepherd's hut. This is an odd sort of king, this wheat-colored, earth-colored, sad-eyed child, laid in a manger but lit by the Eastern star. Is this the king of glory?

Later we saw him riding into Jerusalem. People were waving palms, shouting "Hosanna!" and singing: "Blessed is he who comes in the name of the Lord!" He came into Jerusalem with great celebration. He was acclaimed king, yet he came riding on a donkey. Hardly the animal of choice for a great monarch. Who is this king of glory?

Do you remember? We saw him again a few days afterward. He was standing before Pilate, who mocked him. "So, are *you* the king of the Jews?" You who are crowned with thorns, holding a flimsy reed, the one about to be killed as a common criminal? No wonder Pilate was so scornful of this failure of a man. Is this the king of glory?

But once more we saw him. And at last we understood that this child with hands of the poor; this tortured, mocked, despised man; was indeed the king of glory. For after Jesus' being crucified and buried, God raised him up "and seated him at his right hand in the heavenly places, far above all rule and authority and power and dominion, and above every name that is named" (Ephesians 1:20-21). Now with wonder we proclaim: "At the name of Jesus, every knee shall bow, and every tongue confess him King of glory."

The king to whom every knee bows today is none other than the poor one, the mocked and despised one, who came to be with the least of these, that they might be raised to glory. The head "crowned with many crowns" still bears the marks of the thorns. The feet at which all rulers of the earth will worship are still pierced with nails. This is the peculiar nature of Christ's kingship.

If Jesus Christ is this kind of king, then the last judgment in Matthew cannot be primarily about casting goats into eternal punishment. The Christ who sits on the throne judging the nations is no cruel despot. The judgment may be chilling to those of us who hear the plaintive cries: "Lord, when was it that we saw you hungry or thirsty or a stranger or naked or sick or in prison, and did not take care of you?" (Matthew 25:44). Nevertheless, this judgment is good news for two reasons.

First, Christ the king cares about the "least of these." We may cringe at the image of some being cast into eternal fire, but the point is that Jesus Christ has special concern for the powerless and how they are treated. Our actions count for something. This does not mean that we can earn salvation, but it does mean that the smallest kindness, even if ignored by society, is noticed by Christ. More than this, the smallest kindness, even if ignored by society, is *done* for Christ. Better to live in this kind of cosmos than to dwell in a world where cruelty and kindness have the same ultimate reward.

Second, this judgment is good news because the judge is also redeemer. The one who sits on the throne also came to rescue us from our sins. This is good news, for we are not necessarily among the righteous in the story. We walk by the hungry on our way to buy groceries. We drive past those shivering in the cold on our way home from work. If this judgment scene from Matthew were all we knew of Christ, we would be doomed. But this judge, this king of the poor and hungry, reaches right down even to us, to heal us of our self-importance, to rescue us from our narrow view of the world, to turn us around and offer us new life. This king shows us that we, even we, are among the least of these whom Christ came to save. Thanks be to God.

How do we serve this king? By looking for him among the sick, the hungry, the desperate—the least of these. The three kings in *Amahl and the Night Visitors* may have brought gold, frankincense, and myrrh to Jesus at his birth, but even they admitted that the child didn't need gold or a crown, but that love alone would be the foundation for his kingdom, and the poor would hold the keys to his city.

The one who rules over all dwells with the least of all. This is the heart of the gospel. To this king be all honor and glory, now and forever.

# SUGGESTIONS FOR WORSHIP

## Prayer of Confession

Lord, we confess that we have passed by the hungry and thirsty;
we have not welcomed the stranger,
clothed the naked,
cared for the sick,
or visited those in prison.
We have looked for you where it is comfortable
and have not recognized your face among the poor and suffering.
Lord, have mercy.

## Assurance of Pardon

The good news is this:
the one who comes as judge comes also as redeemer.
Rather than condemnation, he has brought forgiveness.
Rather than destroying us, he has given us new life.
Rather than casting us out, he has welcomed us home.
Friends, believe this good news: in Jesus Christ we are forgiven.

# Contributors

**Denise Bennett** is a professional storyteller and part-time chaplain at the Hermitage United Methodist Home in Richmond, Virginia. She tells all kinds of stories to all kinds of folk in churches, schools, libraries, and festivals throughout Virginia. She also leads retreats and workshops on storytelling, Celtic Christianity, and prayer. Denise is a member of the Tell Tale Hearts Storytellers Theater, a troupe of storytellers who perform regularly at the Glen Allen (Virginia) Cultural Arts Center. In her spare time she loves to walk down by the James River with her husband, Jim, her sons Joshua and James, and their big mutt, Sophie.

**Donna Hopkins Britt** is senior pastor of Calvary Baptist Church in Roanoke, Virginia. In 1994, Donna received the Chevis and Helen Horne Preaching Award at Baptist Theological Seminary at Richmond, Virginia. Several of her writings have appeared in *Homily Service*, a publication of the Liturgical Conference. Donna shares life in Roanoke with her supportive husband, Brian, and their son Noah.

**Katie Geneva Cannon** is the Annie Scales Rogers Professor of Christian Ethics at Union Theological Seminary and the Presbyterian School of Christian Education. Prior to her present position, she served on the faculties of Temple University and the Episcopal Divinity School in Cambridge, Massachusetts. She was the first African American woman ordained in the United Presbyterian Church (USA). The author or editor of several books, including *Katie's Canon: Womanism and the Soul of the Black Community* (Continuum), *Black Womanist Ethics* (American Academy of Religion), and *Teaching Preaching: Isaac Rufus Clark and Black Sacred Rhetoric* (Continuum), she is a nationally known lecturer on theological and ethical topics. Katie is a participant in a pan-African scholars' research seminar on religion and poverty in Africa and the African Diaspora, sponsored by the Ford Foundation.

**Celestine (Tina) Cox** is pastor of the historic Gordonsville Presbyterian Church outside Charlottesville, Virginia. She previously served as an associate pastor of First Presbyterian Church, Charlottesville. When she is not fully engaged with pastoral responsibilities, she works on women's and peacemaking issues. She also spends as much time as possible with her husband, Irv, and their three daughters.

**Jill Y. Crainshaw** is Associate Dean of Vocational Formation and Assistant Professor of Ministerial Studies at the Wake Forest University Divinity School. She is codirector of the Institute for Vocation and Ministry, and program director for the Lilly Grant for Theological Exploration of Vocation. Jill is an ordained minister in the Presbyterian Church (USA), and served churches in North Carolina and Virginia. She is the author of *Wise and Discerning Hearts: An Introduction to Wisdom Liturgical Theology* (The Liturgical Press).

**Lillian Daniel** is the senior minister of the Church of the Redeemer, United Church of Christ, in New Haven, Connecticut, and a lecturer in homiletics at Yale Divinity School. Lillian is a founding member and board chair of the Connecticut Center for a New Economy, which seeks to bring together leaders in religion, community organizing, and labor to act on issues of economic justice. Yale Divinity School, her alma mater, awarded her the Coffin-Forsberg Fellowship for social justice ministry. Currently, she is a member of the Duke Excellence in Ministry Colloquium. She has written for *Christian Century* and *Biblical Preaching Journal*.

**Stacey Simpson Duke** is copastor of First Baptist Church (American Baptist Convention) of Ann Arbor, Michigan, and campus minister for the American Baptist Campus Foundation at the University of Michigan. For five years prior to serving First Baptist, she served as pastor of Fellowship Baptist Church in Edison, Georgia. During her tenure there, by a study funded by the Lilly Endowment, the church was named one of three hundred excellent Protestant congregations in the nation. Stacey is married to her copastor, Paul Simpson Duke. They live in Ann Arbor with two cats and "his and hers" dogs. In addition to caring for their menagerie, Stacey enjoys cooking, reading, hiking, and playing the guitar.

**Tracy Hartman** is Assistant Professor of Practical Theology at the Baptist Theological Seminary at Richmond, and Associate Director of the seminary's Chevis Horne Center for Preaching and Worship. An ordained Baptist minister, she has served as an interim pastor. She has written for several preaching resources and has contributed to the past several volumes of the *Abingdon Preaching Annual*. Tracy lives in Richmond with her husband and two children.

**M. Jan Holton** is ordained in The United Methodist Church. She is completing her Ph.D. in religion and personality at Vanderbilt University in Nashville, Tennessee. Her areas of ministry and research include hospital chaplaincy, crisis counseling, and providing therapeutic care to refugee communities who have suffered psychological trauma due to war and violence.

**Margaret Grun Kibben** is an officer and chaplain in the United States Navy and a minister in the Presbyterian Church (USA). In her present assignment she is serving as chaplain for the Navy's Third Fleet. On active duty in the Navy since 1986, Margaret has had assignments in Quantico, Virginia; the Naval Academy in Annapolis, Maryland; on board ship in Norfolk, Virginia; and with the Marines in Camp Lejeune, North Carolina. She is married to Lieutenant Colonel Timothy J. Kibben, USMC. They live in California with their pride and joy, daughter Lindsay Elizabeth.

**Margaret (Maggie) Palmer Lauterer** is pastor of the First Presbyterian Church of Burnsville in the mountains of North Carolina. Before her career in ministry, Maggie was a newspaper and television journalist and congressional candidate. She is seventh-generation Appalachian and celebrates those roots. She believes the gifts of mountain storytelling and music are perfect ways to tell The Story. Maggie is married to a great guy named Zack and has two wonderful adult children, Selena and Jon. And then there's Olive—the dearest little granddaughter in the world.

**Vicki G. Lumpkin** is the pastor of CityChurch: A Baptist Community of Grace, a new church meeting in the Uptown area of Dallas, Texas. She is a graduate of the Baptist Theological Seminary at Richmond and Union-PSCE, and holds a Ph.D. in practical theology. In her spare time she enjoys visiting and photographing Christian worship space. She is married to the Reverend Charles D. Lumpkin.

**Barbara J. MacHaffie** is Professor of Religion and History at Marietta College, Marietta, Ohio. She is the author of several articles and two books, *Her Story: Women in Christian Tradition* and *Readings in Her Story* (both published by Fortress Press). Her divinity and doctoral degrees are from the University of Edinburgh in Scotland where she lived for five years. She continues her interest in things Scottish by researching and teaching Scottish history. She lives in Marietta with her husband, Fraser, and enjoys reading and traveling.

**Martha L. Moore-Keish** is an Assistant Professor of Liturgical Studies at Yale Divinity School and the Yale Institute of Sacred Music. She holds a Ph.D. in theology from Emory University and is an ordained minister in the Presbyterian Church. She and her husband, Chris, have two daughters, Miriam and Fiona.

**Claire Annelise Smith** is an ordained minister in the Guyana Congregational Union. She served as youth coordinator of the denomination for ten years and as convener of the Mission Education Unit. Her responsibilities included coordinating programs, conducting training events, and writing resource materials. She served on her denomination's Council for World Mission, and the Caribbean and North America Council for Mission. Claire is completing a Ph.D. in education, with a focus on education and mission, how the two complement each other, and the integral role they play in the life of the church. Her hobbies include reading and writing poetry, some of which has been published.

**Susan Steinberg** is Director of Children's Ministries at the United Church of Chapel Hill (UCC) in Chapel Hill, North Carolina. She is an ordained minister in the Presbyterian Church (USA). Prior to her present position she served as interim Presbyterian campus minister at Vanderbilt University in Nashville, Tennessee; as associate pastor of Westminster Presbyterian Church in Charlottesville, Virginia, where she continued her work in campus ministry; and as an interim campus minister for Duke University. She and her husband and two young children live in Chapel Hill, where her husband serves as an admissions officer at the University of North Carolina.

**Beverly A. Zink-Sawyer** is Associate Professor of Preaching and Worship at Union Theological Seminary, and the Presbyterian School of Christian Education in Richmond, Virginia. A minister in the Presbyterian Church (USA), she served churches in Pennsylvania and Tennessee for fifteen years. She is the author of *From Preachers to Suffragists: Woman's Rights and Religious Conviction in the Lives of Three Nineteenth-Century American Clergywomen* (Westminster John Knox Press). She enjoys life in Richmond with her wonderful husband, Steve, and their feline "child" Charis.

# Index

## Subject Index

# Index

## Scripture Index

162